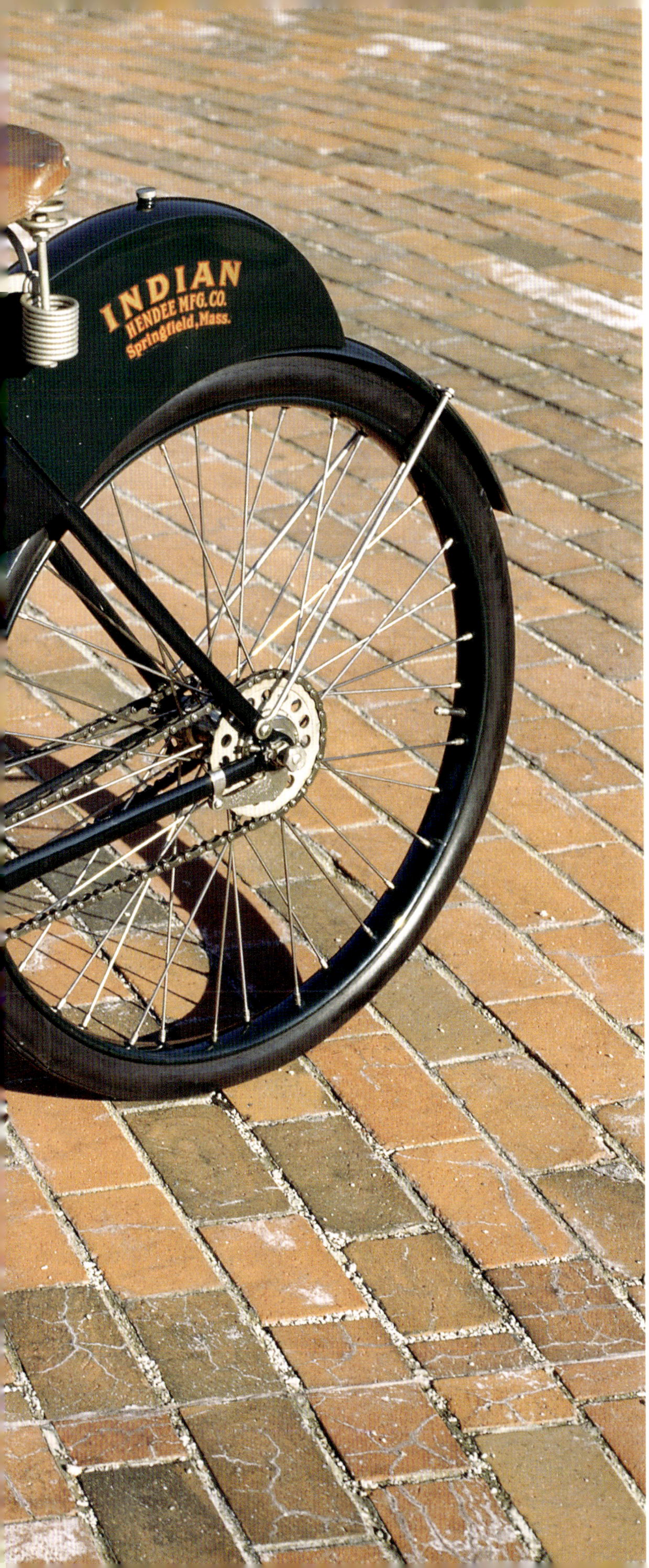

# A Century of INDIAN

Ed Youngblood

First published in 2001 by MBI Publishing Company
Galtier Plaza, Suite 200, 380 Jackson Street,
St. Paul, MN 55101-3885 USA

© Ed Youngblood, 2001
Motorcycle Hall of Fame Museum

All rights reserved. With the exception of quoting brief passages for the purposes of review, no part of this publication may be reproduced without prior written permission from the Publisher.

The information in this book is true and complete to the best of our knowledge. All recommendations are made without any guarantee on the part of the author or Publisher, who also disclaim any liability incurred in connection with the use of this data or specific details.

We recognize that some words, model names and designations, for example, mentioned herein are the property of the trademark holder. We use them for identification purposes only. This is not an official publication.

Motorbooks International Wholesalers & Distributors
Galtier Plaza, Suite 200, 380 Jackson Street,
St. Paul, MN 55101-3885 USA

Library of Congress Cataloging-in-Publication Data available

ISBN 0-7603-1105-6

**On the front cover:** In the early part of the century, board track racing was enormously popular. It began on the small, steeply banked motordromes, which were not much larger than bicycle velodromes. The racing was fast, close, and exciting, but very dangerous. Promoter Jack Prince, who had built most of the wooden tracks around the nation, also created some board tracks as big as two miles in length, intended for car racing. Motorcycles were capable of very high speeds on the boards. For example, in 1926 Curly Fredricks set a board track record of 120.3 miles per hour aboard a 61-ci. (1,000-cc) side valve Indian. Pictured is a 1912 eight-valve factory board track racer owned by John Parham

**On the frontispiece:** An advertisement from the late 1920s

**On the title page:** By 1905, Indian had produced over 1,000 motorcycles, and in that year some significant changes were made in the design. The rigid front bicycle-type fork was replaced with cartridge-spring suspension, and a twist grip control throttle was introduced. Indian's standard color was blue. Red—or vermilion—appeared as an option in 1903, and green was added to the color choices in 1905. This 1905 Indian single is owned by Mort Wood

**On the back cover:** *Top Left:* Ralph Hepburn won championships for both Indian and Harley-Davidson. *Don Emde Productions*

*Top Right:* As Indian emerged from World War II, only the Chief remained in its product line. Projects begun during the final years of the du Pont administration—such as a new in-line four and a shaft-drive, foot-shift V-twin—were shelved by the new Rogers regime. For 1947, the aging Chief offered only minor changes, such as a return to the Indian head fender light and the script logo on the tank. Remarkably, sales were nearly four-times the previous season, rising to nearly 12,000 units. With Harley-Davidson selling just 20,000 units that year, the 1947 Chief proved it still had significant customer appeal.

*Bottom Left:* A 1925 advertisement for the Prince

*Bottom Right:* A 1949 Scout owned by Greg Easley of Johnson City, Tennessee

**Endpaper:** 1949 Scout owned by Greg Easley, 1905 Indian single owned by Mort Wood, Arrow Streamliner owned by Harold Parks, and 1912 eight-valve factory board track racer owned by John Parham.

Edited by Darwin Holmstrom
Designed by Tom Heffron

Printed in Hong Kong

# CONTENTS

Acknowledgments 6

Introduction 7

The Story of Indian 8

Indian Archive 70

Exhibit Gallery 92

George Hendee: In His Own Words 160

Index 168

# ACKNOWLEDGMENTS

For their advice, guidance, moral support, and assistance with research, I would like to thank Steve Adams, Glenn Bator, Henry Bernstein, June Cook, Donald Davidson, Everitt du Pont, Don Emde, Larry Feece, Peter Gagan, Allan Girdler, Jeff Glasserow, Rocky Halter, Ernie Hartman, Jerry Hatfield, Darwin Holmstrom, Guy Jones, Bruce Linsday, Robin Markey, Mark Mederski, Katy Nastali, Christie Obata, Harold Parks, Dr. John Patt, Bob Shingler, Doug Strange, Mort Wood, and George Yarocki.

I would also like to thank the Motorcycle Hall of Fame Museum, located in Pickerington, Ohio, for putting together this historic collection of Indian motorcycles, and helping to preserve the heritage of this remarkable brand. The museum tells the stories that make up the history of motorcycling through exhibits such as this, as well as through a wide range of other displays and exhibits. To learn more about the museum, please visit its website at: www.motorcyclemuseum.org

# INTRODUCTION

A century ago, the Hendee Manufacturing Company of Springfield, Massachusetts, began to build and sell a motorcycle named Indian. Although very little more in the beginning than a motor-assisted bicycle, within a decade, Indian became a marque recognized and respected throughout the industrialized world. Its sales in America and Europe turned the Hendee Manufacturing Company, and later the Indian Motocycle Company, into an industrial giant, dominant within the American motorcycle market.

In its first two decades, the Indian established its reputation for leading-edge design, durability, and quality. Later it set new standards for style and beauty. Its gracefully curved sheet metal made it to motorcycles what the Chrysler building is to architecture, and what the Auburn was to automobiles. Even people who knew very little about motorcycles knew an Indian when they saw one. And, in most cases, they adored it.

Even today, with the original manufacturer defunct for almost a half-century, Indian is recognized as motorcycling's class act to the extent that both scalawags and honest men have spent fortunes battling over the right to control the trademark. Again and again, parties on several continents have attempted to resurrect the proud Indian name and emblazon it on the gas tank of a new motorcycle.

In celebration of a the 100th anniversary of Indian motorcycles, this book, in cooperation with "A Century of Indian, presented by Progressive Insurance" at the Motorcycle Hall of Fame Museum, will present an overview of the fascinating story of Indian. Others more expert than I—Paul Brokaw, Allan Girdler, Jerry Hatfield, Ted Hodgdon, Thomas Firth Jones, John J. O'Connor, Harry Sucher, George Yarocki, and others—have already chronicled the story of Indian in greater detail. I am indebted to them and need not attempt to duplicate their efforts. Besides, while words can tell the story of the brand, there may be no better way to really appreciate the Indian than through its visual image. Many of the images in this book are motorcycles on display in the Century of Indian exhibit at the Motorcycle Hall of Fame Museum. They demonstrate that in its beauty, its style, its grace, and its rainbow of colors, there has never been—and may never be again—a mass-produced motorcycle quite as handsome as the Indian.

—*Ed Youngblood*
*Curator*
*A Century of Indian*
*The Motorcycle Hall of Fame Museum*

# THE STORY OF INDIAN

**1904 INDIAN SINGLE**

*The Indian Motocycle Company emerged from a one-page agreement between George Hendee and Oscar Hedstrom in January 1901. Hedstrom, a self-taught engineer, had previously built reliable single-cylinder motorcycles designed for pacing bicycle races. Not only were his engines reliable, but he designed a superior carburetor that provided smooth and controllable operation. Hendee believed it was time to mass produce a motor-assisted bicycle for the public at large. Hedstrom's first prototype appeared in May 1901, and in 1902 the Hendee Manufacturing Company built and sold 143 Indian motorcycles. For many years demand outpaced production, and Indian grew to become the largest motorcycle manufacturer in the world. Because Hendee's small factory could not keep up with demand, for the first five years Indian had its Hedstrom engines built by the Aurora Automatic Machinery Company of Aurora, Illinois. This example of a 1904 Indian has appeared previously at the Motorcycle Hall of Fame Museum. It was restored by Bud Ekins for the Steve McQueen collection. Later purchased at auction by Butch Baer, it was donated to the Motorcycle Hall of Fame Museum, then given to the Federation Internationale de Motocyclisme in Geneva, Switzerland.*

# THE BIRTH OF THE BRAND

George Hendee, born in Watertown, Connecticut in 1866, took up bicycle racing at the age of 16, prior to the advent of the modern "safety" bicycle. Hendee raced the old nineteenth century high wheelers with extraordinary success, and won his first national championship in 1881 at Hampden Park in Springfield, Massachusetts. According to an account published in *The Motorcyclist,* "He continued his undefeated reign until 1886, when he retired unbeaten, the holder of many national titles and all high wheel records from 1 to 20 miles." Actually, he did not retire from racing "unbeaten," though his record was astonishing, winning 302 races out of 309 starts.

Following his successful racing career, Hendee moved into the bicycle trade as a salesman, later became a dealer, and in 1889 formed the Hendee Manufacturing Company to produce Silver King and Silver Queen brand bicycles. During this period, the old high wheel design—which could be operated by only the most athletically inclined—was giving way to the new safety bicycle introduced by Rover in England in 1885. The safety bicycle, which featured a steerable front wheel, wheels of equal size, and a pedal-and-crank drive to the rear wheel in the middle, brought bicycling into widespread popularity. It was a vehicle that both women and men could enjoy without much fear of embarrassment or injury. Its influence cannot be overstated. Aside from relying on a horse, prior to the invention of the safety bicycle, most people got from place to place by walking. This new, easy-to-operate machine became enormously popular as personal transportation.

Born in Sweden in 1871, Oscar Hedstrom and his family emigrated to the United States and settled in Brooklyn in 1880. At 16, Hedstrom apprenticed himself to a watchmaking company, where he learned about machine tools, pattern making, and foundry work. In 1899 he obtained a French De Dion engine, and by studying that simple engine, he found that he could make improvements that would substantially increase performance and dependability. His work on this engine along with his experience with watch making, machine tools, pattern making, and foundry work put him in the category of a self-trained mechanical engineer.

A whole new form of racing was developing around the swift and agile safety-style bicycles. On these machines, athletic young men attained high speeds—sometimes for sustained periods—on indoor and outdoor wooden banked tracks called velodromes, designed specifically for bicycle racing. In some cases motorized bicycles—called pacers—were used to run ahead of the bicycle racers to break the air and reduce wind resistance.

Visionary inventors on both sides of the Atlantic had been trying to create bicycle-like motorized vehicles since the mid-nineteenth century, even before the invention of the gasoline engine. A Massachusetts inventor named Sylvester Roper built a practical steam-powered two-wheeler as early as 1867. Almost simultaneously, the steam-powered Michaux-Perreux was invented in France. Historians still disagree about which machine came first.

The first practical application of a gasoline engine (patented by Dr. Nicholas Otto in 1876) to a two-wheeled vehicle came in 1885 in Germany when Gottlieb Daimler successfully operated his wooden-framed "Boneshaker." Daimler did not have the slightest intention of creating a motorcycle. All he wanted was a rolling test bed for engine development, but what he came up with coincidentally followed modern motorcycle design. He went on to form the transportation giant Daimler-Benz.

For the next decade, inventors experimented with all kinds of motorized vehicles, but it was the partnership of Count Albert De Dion and Georges Bouton in France in 1884 that developed an engine so practical for application to bicycle chassis that it was quickly copied all over the industrialized world. The De Dion engine was a small single-cylinder configuration that developed about a half-horsepower. Its success can be credited largely to the innovation of combustion chamber ignition through an electric spark. Another problem with early gasoline engines was how to effectively atomize the fuel to create a controlled and consistent fuel/air mixture. Oscar Hedstrom's tinkering with the De Dion engine led to improvements in this area. Much of Oscar Hedstrom's—and Indian's—early success can be attributed to the fact that he developed a superior carburetor.

It is not likely that by 1900 Hedstrom had planned to play a part in putting the world on wheels. He wanted to build a fast and reliable pacer to use at bicycle races. The early pacers were notoriously unreliable, and press accounts of the day report the ridicule and delight of the fans when a smoking, coughing, sputtering pacer was overtaken and passed by the bicycle racers. This did not happen with Hedstrom's machine. It worked and kept working.

Noting the successful performance of the Hedstrom pacers, George Hendee approached him in the fall of 1900 with the idea of designing a motor-assisted bicycle that could be mass produced and sold to the public at large. An agreement was reached between the two in January 1901. On May 25, 1901, a prototype motor-bicycle powered

PAGE 9:
**EARLY SUCCESS**
*By the end of its first year of production, the Hendee Manufacturing Company knew it had a successful product in its Indian "motocycle." With a dealer network developing, Indian produced this catalog in 1903. Characteristically, the company's early literature is attractive and top quality.*

**INDIAN UTILITY AND VERSATILITY**

*This picture from the 1906 catalog promotes the Indian's utility and versatility. In addition to the standard two-wheeler, there are the Tandem, the Triplet, the Tri-Car, the Tricycle, and the Van.*

by a Hedstrom engine was demonstrated on the streets of Springfield, including the Cross Street hill, which was the steepest hill in the city. Two more machines were built in 1901, but mass production did not begin until 1902. This new motorcycle—or called by some a "motocycle"—was named "Indian," a brand name that had already achieved commercial success at Hendee Manufacturing.

By 1897 the Hendee Manufacturing company was producing 4,000 bicycles per year, some of which were intended for export. These export products were called "nameplate" bicycles because export commission firms placing an order of 100 or more selected a brand name, which was installed as a nameplate on Hendee's basic Silver King design. As export sales grew, Hendee soon found it a nuisance to create different nameplates for each exporter, and he finally decided that he would provide one brand only for the overseas market, and it would be called "American Indian."

Explaining the history of the marque in picturesque language, Hendee wrote, "Soon I realized that in the name 'Indian' we had a winner for bicycles. When the motorcycle came along a year or so later, it simply was out of the question to think of calling it anything but Indian. This name fitted the motorcycle even better than it did the bicycle, and before many moons had passed, the new warrior had deposed the old chief altogether from the wigwam. That is why there is an Indian motorcycle today."

Incidentally, these events took place at the small Hendee factory on Worthington Street in downtown Springfield. Later, when Hendee Manufacturing moved to a new site and began to construct a larger factory at State Street and Wilbraham Road, it became officially known as the "Wigwam." Consistent with company nomenclature, Hendee was known as the Chief, and Hedstrom was called the Medicine Man, in respect to his mechanical wizardry. In flowery language characteristic of the era, John O'Connor, who served as Indian's advertising man from 1901 to 1915, wrote of Indian's dealer network as its "tribe," and of its worldwide sphere of influence as Indian's "nation."

Indian further distinguished itself by not using the term "motorcycle" in its company name. Rather, it was "the Indian Motocycle Company," dropping the "r" in the word "motorcycle." "Motocycle" was an archaic word that had appeared in the late nineteenth century to describe the new motor-driven vehicles that were also called "horseless carriages." Although "Indian Motocycle Company" was used for marketing and promotional purposes from the outset, it was not until 1923 that the corporation formally changed its name from the Hendee Manufacturing Company to the Indian Motocycle Company.

It did not take long to realize that the Worthington Street factory was not adequate to produce Hedstrom engines in the quantity that would be required. Consequently, in October 1901, an agreement was signed with the Aurora Automatic Machinery Company of Aurora, Illinois, to build engines for Indian. Under this agreement, Aurora supplied Indian with Hedstrom engines, but it was also licensed to build and sell an engine known as the Thor and based on the Hedstrom design to other fledgling motorcycle manufacturers. Oscar Hedstrom moved to Aurora to continue engine development and to oversee manufacturing and quality control. Building its own rolling chassis in Springfield to carry the Aurora-built Hedstrom engines, Indian sold 143 motorcycles in its first model year.

In 1903, Indian produced and sold 376 motorcycles. But thanks to the licensing agreement with Aurora, and thanks to a general proliferation of De Dion–type engines throughout America, practically any person who had a bicycle shop and was so inclined strapped a single-cylinder engine to a bicycle frame and became a motorcycle manufacturer. Some historians have identified as many as 200 brands made in America prior to 1920. Some of these appeared in very small quantities, and some were reasonably frank copies of the Indian motorcycle. Indian's greatest early competitors were Orient, Auto-Bi, America Light, Pope, Thor, Crescent, Imperial, Monarch, and Warwick, some of which were powered by the Aurora engine of Oscar Hedstrom's design.

**INDIAN SIDECARS**

*Prior to the Ford's dominance of the personal transportation market in the middle teens, American motorcycle manufacturers—including Indian—enjoyed a vigorous demand for sidecars. A number of independent sidecar manufacturers thrived, such as the famous Flxible Sidecar Company of Loudonville, Ohio. After Henry Ford improved the efficiency of Model T production and made his cars more affordable through an installment credit plan, the popularity of motorcycle sidecars began to wane. Throughout its history, Indian manufactured its own sidecars. This example is attached to a 1913 twin. Owned by William Eggers, it has previously appeared at the Motorcycle Hall of Fame Museum.*

### 1914 HENDEE SPECIAL

*By 1913, Indian was producing over 30,000 units per year. Its popularity was driven by its reputation for reliability, but the company was also noted for innovation and technology. Undoubtedly its most innovative technological step to date was the Hendee Special, a motorcycle with an electric starter introduced in 1914. The idea and the mechanical engineering of this vehicle were sound, but battery technology of the day was not up to providing the necessary energy for day-to-day operation. The Hendee Special was a technical failure, representing an idea ahead of its time. It was offered only in 1914, then dropped from the model line. This Hendee Special pictured is an original, unrestored example owned by William Scott.*

Indian's greatest single competitor at the time was the Marsh motorcycle, manufactured by the Atlantic Automobile Company in Brockton, Massachusetts.

In the meantime, Indian's greatest ultimate rival, the Harley-Davidson, emerged in 1903 from a small shed in Milwaukee, Wisconsin. But at the time, the booming American motorcycle industry gave little notice to what was just another obscure brand among many. Indian was quickly becoming the recognized chief of an ever-growing tribe of motorized two-wheelers.

By 1905, Indian production was up to over 1,000 units a year, and the marque had begun to distinguish itself for its reliability. Unlike many motorcycles of the era that had a leather belt drive to the rear wheel, Indian had a chain drive that would not slip on steep hills or under wet riding conditions. Being competitive by nature, George Hendee immediately sought out opportunities to prove his motorcycle. The Indian won its first public competition in July 1902, in an endurance ride from Boston to New York City. Sometimes Hendee personally carried the company banner in these events. At

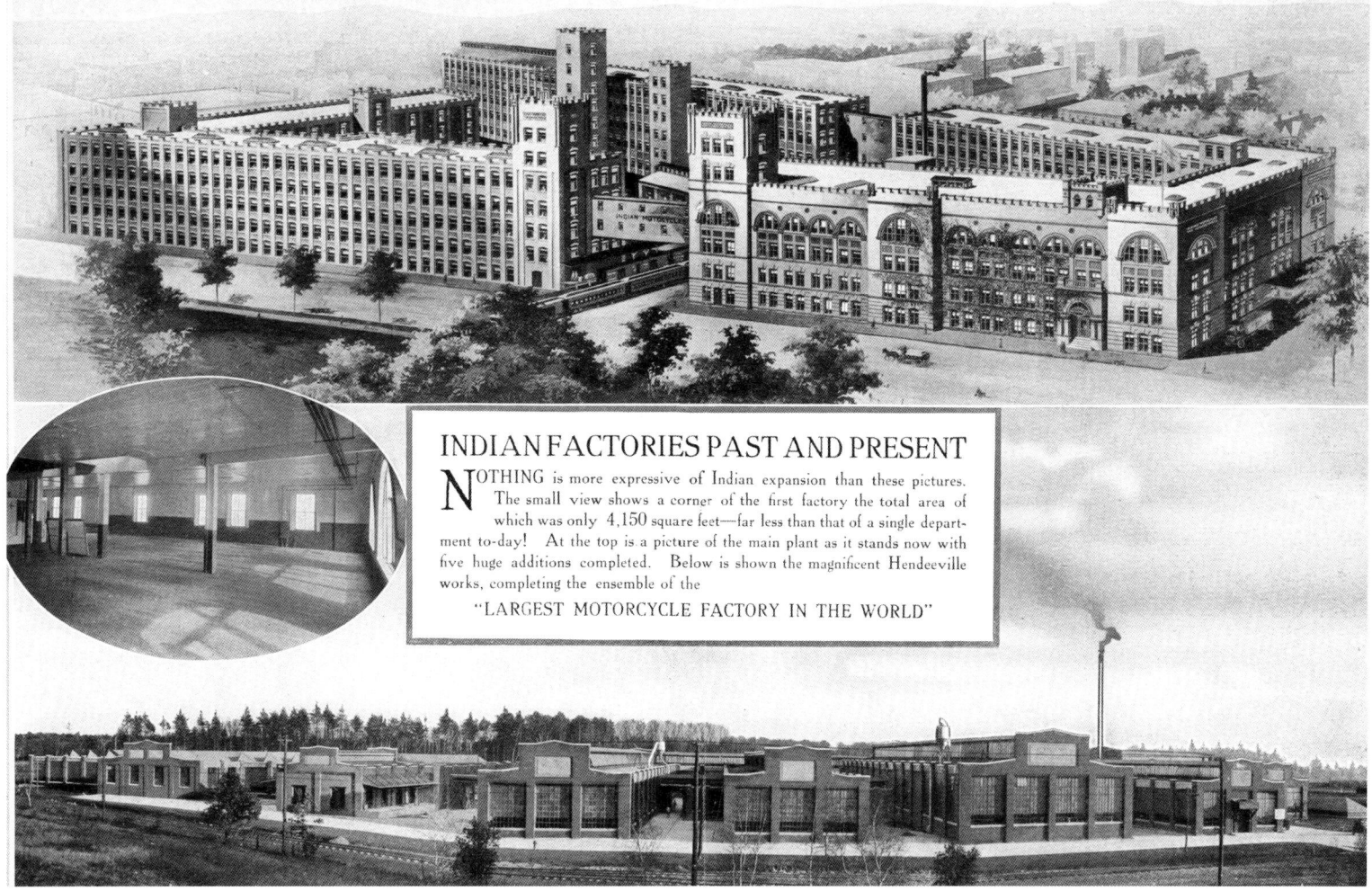

**INDIAN FACTORIES PAST AND PRESENT**

NOTHING is more expressive of Indian expansion than these pictures. The small view shows a corner of the first factory the total area of which was only 4,150 square feet—far less than that of a single department to-day! At the top is a picture of the main plant as it stands now with five huge additions completed. Below is shown the magnificent Hendeeville works, completing the ensemble of the

"LARGEST MOTORCYCLE FACTORY IN THE WORLD"

one difficult endurance event during 1903, Hendee finished with his hands bruised and bleeding, battered from holding onto the handlebars over rough cobblestone streets. The little motorcycle invariably demonstrated its toughness, but it did not provide much comfort for its rider. Consequently, in 1905 the conventional rigid bicycle front fork was replaced with Indian's cartridge-spring suspension. In 1905, Indian also built its first twin-cylinder engines, but they were produced in very limited quantities and for racing purposes only.

In 1907, Indian took a big step in its commitment to compete in the vigorous and growing American motorcycle industry. It introduced a 38-ci (633-cc) V-twin engine, and relocated its factory to what would become the eventual site of the sprawling Wigwam. Indian also canceled its contract with Aurora in October 1906, in preparation for undertaking its own engine production for the 1907 model year. With total production under its control, Indian built over 3,000 motorcycles in 1908, adding to a lifetime production that was approaching 15,000 units. At peak efficiency, the factory could turn out a new Indian every 15 minutes, or 30 motorcycles per shift. No other American brand was even close to this level of production.

In 1908, Indian introduced what—in retrospect—might be considered the motorcycle industry's first "sport bike," although that term would not come into common

**THE WIGWAM TAKES SHAPE**

*In its 1911 sales catalog, Indian depicts its expanded factory, not yet complete but well under way. The brochure boasts of the Wigwam's more than three acres of floor space. Indian motorcycles began life at a small factory on Worthington Street in downtown Springfield, Massachusetts. At first the Hedstrom engines were supplied under contract by the Aurora Automatic Machinery Company. With sales rapidly growing, Indian moved to a 74,000-square-foot facility at 837 State Street in Springfield, Massachusetts, in 1906. With its 1907 model year, the motorcycle—including the engine—was manufactured entirely at the Springfield facility. By the time expansion ended in 1919, the Wigwam had more than 400,000 square feet, or over nine acres of floor space, in its five-story structure. Theoretically the plant was capable of producing 60,000 motorcycles per year, although actual production reached a little more than half that number in 1913, Indian's best year.*

**INDIAN'S INDUSTRIAL MIGHT**
*Indian had undisputed bragging rights over all of its competitors, domestic or foreign, in its manufacturing capability. This was emphasized in high-quality and lavishly printed promotional literature like the 1919 booklet entitled "Selling Support," distributed to motorcycle dealers.*

usage for another 80 years. This was a single with a 3.5-horsepower engine fitted with a new mechanically actuated intake valve. The "humpback" rear-fender fuel tank seen on previous Indians was replaced with a sleek "torpedo tank" above the main frame bar. The saddle was extended far backward, right over the rear wheel, enabling the rider to crouch down into a wind-cheating racing position. Because of the rider's odd position, some called it Indian's "Monkey-on-a-Stick" motorcycle.

## A Real Motorcycle Appears

With Indian dwarfing its competitors in the American motorcycle market, it seems odd to suggest that it was not—prior to this time—a "real" motorcycle. However, one must recall that the age of motorized travel was still very young and it was only natural that people still thought of their two-wheelers as motor-assisted bicycles. The state-of-the-art product still used conventional pedals for starting, and sometimes to help the motor along under tough going. Many brands—including Indian—were still bicycles by design, utilizing the "diamond" frame of the conventional safety bicycle.

The diamond frame is a parallelogram of tubing that connects four key structural points: the steering head, the mounting point for the seat, the connecting points for the rear axle, and the mounting point for the sprocket and pedals. Between the sprocket mounting point and the seat mounting point is a structural tube that keeps the frame in shape and rigid. Except for the fact that Indian designed its single-cylinder engine to function as this structural unit, very little differed between an Indian and a bicycle, other than the accessories required by the engine, such as a fuel tank, the battery tube, and the electrical coil. It was, in essence, not a vehicle designed around an engine. It was a conventional bicycle to which an engine had been added.

Some companies had already begun to see things differently. For example, as early as 1901, the Werner, built in Paris, featured a frame purposely built to locate the engine down low and in the center of the vehicle. Similarly, Harley-Davidson, not having come out of a bicycling tradition, appeared in 1903 with an engine-cradling frame that positioned the engine similar to the location used in the Werner. With a new factory, its own engine production, and a line that included singles and twins, Indian took this step in 1909 by introducing a robust "loop" frame specifically designed to cradle the engine. This design allowed for the development of larger and heavier engines and lowered the center of gravity, resulting in a faster and more manageable and maneuverable vehicle.

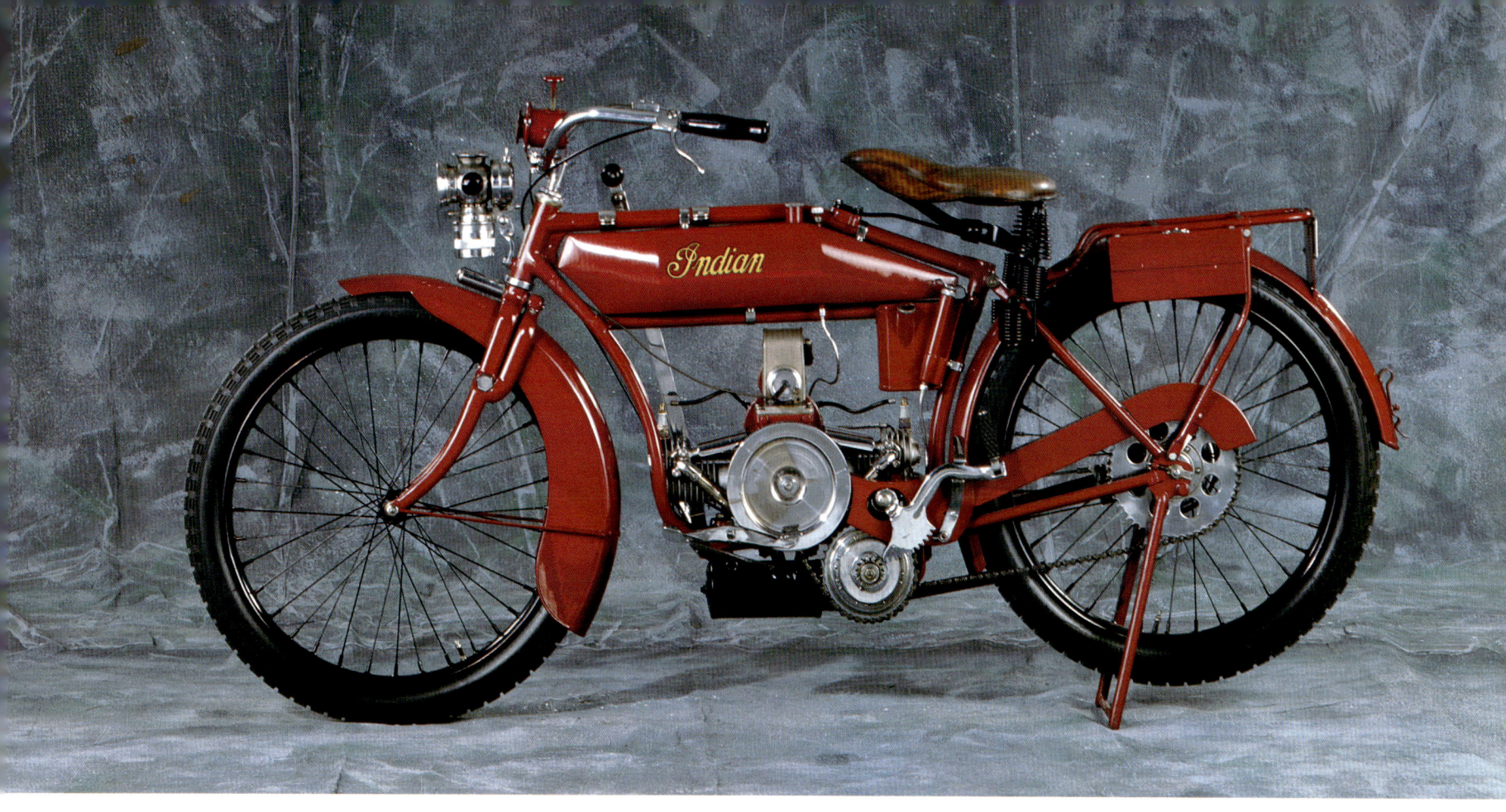

Indian abandoned the concept of a motor-assisted bicycle with the adoption of a loop frame. An automatic oil pump, a leaf-spring front suspension, a two-speed transmission, and a hand-crank starter appeared in 1910. Production increased to over 6,000 units per year. Perhaps symbolic of the marque's growing pride and sense of identity, the legendary Indian script logo also appeared in 1910, heralding the fact that one day Indian would become American motorcycling's benchmark for style and beauty.

The willingness to seek innovative solutions for a better motorcycle was one of the reasons Indian emerged from the pack in the early days of motorcycling. For example, though its use of chain drive from the outset had given it superiority over other brands in reliability competitions, in work-a-day use, the chain drive did not provide as smooth a ride as belt drive. In 1909, Indian experimented with belt drive to the rear wheel, and from 1910 through 1912, produced belt-drive models in limited quantities. Indian did not stick with the system, possibly because it achieved a more civilized ride as early as 1913 with an innovative swinging-arm and leaf-spring rear suspension. Also in 1913, the hand-crank starting system, which was deemed too dangerous, was replaced with a foot starter.

Indian had already begun to develop a growing export business. By the early teens it had 3,000 dealers worldwide, 17 factory branches throughout the United States, branch offices in London and Melbourne, and a factory in Toronto. In 1911 the

**1917 MODEL O**

*By the middle teens, Indian was known for its strong, reliable twin-cylinder motorcycles, a reputation established by its Hedstrom-engined 1,000-cc Big Twins, then subsequently by the 1,000-cc twin-cylinder Powerplus. However, with the outbreak of World War I, the emerging popularity of inexpensive Ford automobiles, and a downturn in the economy, motorcycle sales were leveling off. Indian believed it needed an economy model in its line. It responded in 1916 with the Featherweight, a 221-cc two-stroke single with an external flywheel. Sales for the Featherweight were not good, and in 1917 it was replaced by the Model O, a more sophisticated 257-cc four-stroke twin. The engine, in design and longitudinal placement in the frame, was a lot like the British Douglas motorcycle. The Model O also was not particularly popular, and it stayed in the model line only through 1919. The unfortunate model designation enabled critics to deride it as the "Model Nothing." The Model O pictured is owned by Margaret Camarata.*

## SIDE-VALVE TECHNOLOGY

The side-valve Powerplus, designed by Charles Gustafson, appeared in 1916. It was more economical to manufacture than the F-head Hedstrom engine, and more powerful, due to better combustion chamber efficiency. That same year, Irish racing star Charles Franklin emigrated to America and joined Indian's engineering department. In 1920, Franklin released his own side-valve rendition, the 600-cc Scout. This fantastically successful design became the engineering platform for three decades of future Indians, up to and including the 80-ci Chief. Franklin was so good at coaxing performance out of side-valve engines that his Indians finally made obsolete the eight-valve works racers of other manufacturers.

company confirmed its reputation on an international level by taking the first three places at the famous Isle of Man Senior Tourist Trophy with special machines designed and personally maintained by Oscar Hedstrom. It was the first time that a non-British motorcycle won the Isle of Man, and the only time in history that an American motorcycle has won the legendary event. Thanks to its two-speed gearbox and chain drive, Indians ridden by Englishmen Oliver Godfrey and A. J. Moorehouse, as well as Irishman Charles Franklin, handily outclassed their British competitors, many of which still used belt drive. American Jake DeRosier brought another Indian home in 12th place, having crashed during the race. But DeRosier redeemed himself the following month by setting a record at 87 miles per hour on the famous oval racetrack at Brooklands.

The resounding victory on the Isle of Man and DeRosier's subsequent performance at Brooklands were not Indian's first successful international outings. Privateer T. K. "Teddy" Hastings had scored 994 of a possible 1,000 points aboard the newly introduced Indian twin at the 1907 Thousand Mile Reliability Trial in England. This event was the predecessor of the International Six Days Trial, in which Hastings, in 1908, became the first American to win a medal, this time with support from the Indian factory.

Few realize today that America, in the form of the Federation of American Motorcyclists (FAM) (the predecessor to the American Motorcyclist Association [AMA]), was one of the original 12 members of the Federation of International Motorcycle Clubs (FICM), which was later renamed the FIM (Federation Internationale de Motocyclisme). Such political clout in the international motorcycle sport can be attributed entirely to Indian and its British importer, William H. "Billy" Wells, who represented America to the London-based international federation.

In 1912 the famous Indian Red paint appeared as a standard color, and technical features were added, based on high-performance parts proven on the victorious 1911 Isle of Man works Indians. In 1913 the Cradle Spring Frame was introduced, providing rear suspension on all models. The Cradle Spring Frame was quite sophisticated for its day, featuring a rear swinging arm that enabled the rear wheel to move up and down against chrome vanadium leaf springs extending backward from below the seat.

Sectional View of Powerolus Motor, with Large Valves and Generous Gas Passages. Most Powerful and Economical Motor Ever Fitted in a Motorcycle

In 1912, Indian experienced a racing tragedy that forever changed the motorcycle sport. Evolving from the smaller velodromes built for bicycle racing, wooden "motordromes" had sprung up all over the country. These facilities were banked wooden tracks that generated high speeds and hair-raising competition. Often spectators leaned over the top edge of the track, unprotected from the speeding motorcycles that flashed past. Subject to weather and engine oil, these board tracks tended to become treacherous and dilapidated. The racing was dangerous and a critical press began to call the facilities "murderdromes."

At a race in Newark, New Jersey, in September 1912, professional rider Eddy Hasha's factory-sponsored eight-valve Indian began to malfunction. Losing control, Hasha roared up the banked track to the upper edge, and before his motorcycle came to rest, he and another rider and six spectators were dead or dying. News reports claimed that some of the spectators were decapitated by Hasha's careening machine.

### 1924 CHIEF

*The Scout, introduced in 1920 with a 37-ci (600-cc) engine, had its powerplant enlarged to 61 ci (1,000 cc) in 1922, then to 74 ci (1,200 cc) in 1923. The 1,000-cc model was designated the Chief, and the 1,200 was designated the Big Chief. The motorcycle pictured is a 1924 Chief owned by the Motorcycle Hall of Fame Museum.*

## ACE

*William Henderson is considered by many to be the father of the American four-cylinder motorcycle. His designs influenced several brands, including Indian. William Henderson, in partnership with his brother Thomas, began to build motorcycles in 1912. His fours were long, smooth, and luxurious. In 1917 his company was purchased by Ignaz Schwinn, the producer of Excelsior motorcycles. Henderson did not stay with Schwinn long, but departed to start up a company to produce another four-cylinder motorcycle, the Ace, manufactured in Philadelphia. The Ace established its reputation with speed and endurance records, but could not survive in the recession economy of the 1920s. When Henderson was killed testing one of his motorcycles in 1922, the company struggled on under the guidance of engineer Arthur Lemon. Eventually it was purchased by Michigan Motors, then acquired by Indian in 1927. Indian brought the motorcycle into its product line in 1928 as the Indian Ace. In 1929 it was renamed the Indian Four, initiating an engineering and styling evolution that resulted in what many consider some of the most beautiful motorcycles ever created.*

This brought the motorcycle sport to the front page of *The New York Times,* but not in a way that the industry or its fans would have hoped for. As much as any other single factor, the Hasha crash eventually brought to a close the era of American motordrome motorcycle racing.

In January 1914 the Wigwam outdid itself technically by introducing the Hendee Special, an Indian with electric lighting and an electric starter. While the starting system on the Hendee Special was sound, battery technology had not yet arrived at a level sufficient to drive the starter under daily use. The Hendee Special remained in the model line for only one year, then electric starting disappeared from motorcycling for another four decades.

By the middle teens—a little over a decade after the introduction of the brand—the Indian factory had become an industrial giant, producing over 30,000 motorcycles per year, with half going to overseas markets. These are production numbers that would be envied by some viable companies in the modern motorcycle industry. In 1910, Indian began to expand its original 74,000-square-foot State Street factory. Construction, initially under the supervision of Oscar Hedstrom, continued off and on into 1919, until the Wigwam became a 400,000-square-foot industrial monster capable of producing 60,000 motorcycles per year.

As if joyously and arrogantly celebrating its dominance over the motorcycle industry, about this time the Wigwam introduced its famous "Laughing Indian" logo. Indian racers quickly recognized its usefulness as a psychological weapon, placing it on the back of their riding jerseys to taunt the competition.

Pride and arrogance may also have been exposed in an interesting poster entitled "The Evolution of the Race," produced in 1911, which showed the history of Indian production since 1901. With just under 10,000 units sold in 1911, this poster predicted a near-doubling of sales to 19,500 in 1912, another 80 percent increase to 35,000 in 1913, then another 70 percent increase to 60,000 units in 1914, reaching the full production capability of the Wigwam.

But Indian never came close to the ambitious production capability designed into its huge factory. By 1913 the company had unknowingly already seen its best days. From a high of 32,000 units in 1913, production declined to 25,000 in 1914 and to 21,000 in 1915.

## Indian and Motorcycling Fall on Hard Times

Many current-day riders think of Indian as an old and once-proud American company that began to lose its position in the market with the invasion of British and European motorcycles that followed World War II. In reality, the company actually embarked on a downward trend as early as 1914, and that trend became a painful and interminable slide, exacerbated by poor leadership, unexpected competitive forces, and a worldwide economic crisis.

Erosion in leadership began when Oscar Hedstrom retired in 1913, at the young age of 42. Hedstrom was not only the designer of a simple and reliable engine that carried Indian from inception to success, but he became an accomplished industrial engineer whose talents enabled Indian's production to keep pace with its rapidly growing demand. Hedstrom returned in 1916 to help sort out what had become by then a production department mess, but he did not stay long.

Then in 1915, George Hendee, at the age of 49, stepped away from hands-on management, resigning as general manager but continuing for a short time as president of the company. Then Hendee resigned as president and went into full retirement in 1916, replaced by John F. Alvord. Alvord was also president of the Standard Electric Company and the Edison-Splitdorf Company, and he spent most of his time in his New York offices. Management of the company was largely left to Frank J. Weschler, who had joined Indian in 1905 as a bookkeeper, coming up through the ranks to the position of treasurer under the mentorship of George Hendee.

Following the Hendee/Hedstrom era, the big company fell into the hands of a board of directors who were not always motorcycle people. They lost sight of their core business and

### INDIAN ON THE SIDE OF THE LAW

*Police sales were very important for both Indian and Harley-Davidson. Major city law enforcement agencies were in a position to place large orders, and the company whose motorcycles were chosen gained visibility and prestige. Indian liked to position its police bikes as swift tools against lawlessness. Its advertising department describe its motorcycles as "The speeder's conscience!" Indian's efforts to court police sales are illustrated in this brochure, in addition to the 1924 brochure "Maintaining Law and Order" that appears on page 27 and the 1936 brochure "The Pride of the Force" that apperars on page 37.*

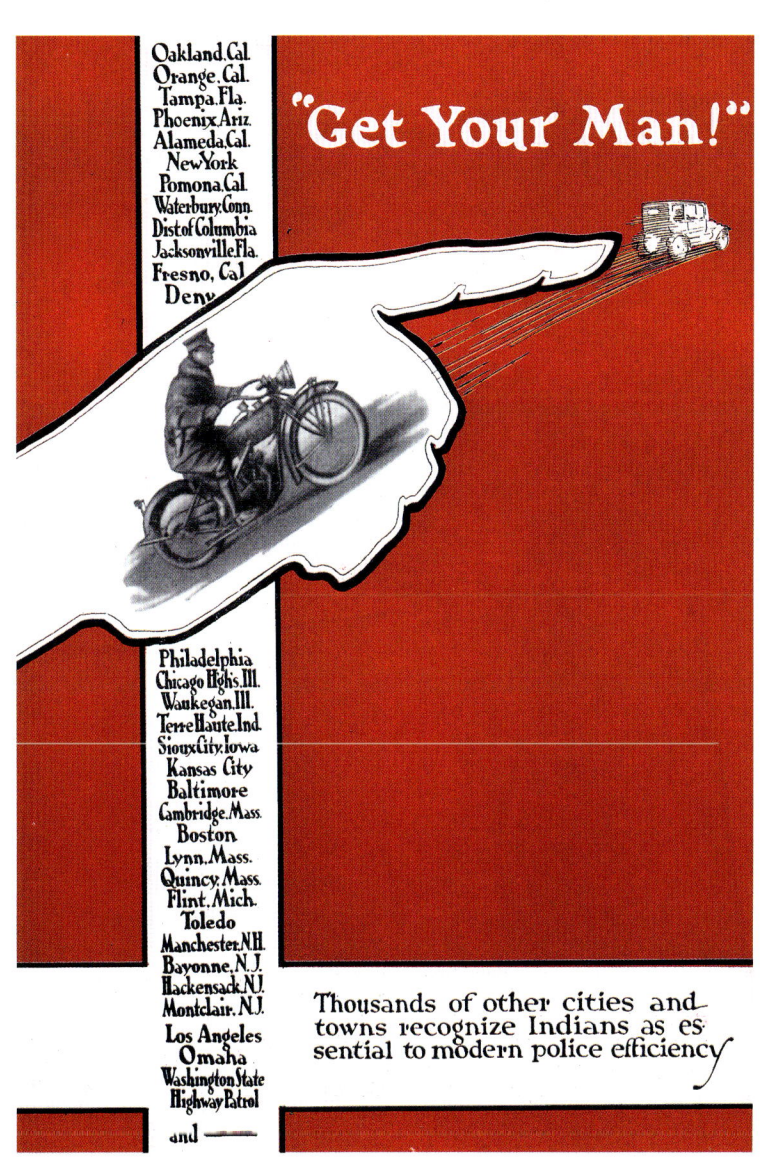

PREVIOUS PAGE SPREAD:

**1927 FACTORY HILLCLIMBER**

*Hillclimbing has always been a popular motorcycling activity, and it became especially popular during the Depression, when both Indian and Harley-Davidson supported the development of special factory hillclimbers. The motorcycle pictured was ridden to AMA amateur hillclimbing national championships from 1927 through 1930 by Bob Armstrong, the son of Earl "Red" Armstrong, legendary Indian track racer, production manager, and lifetime employee. It is powered by an 80-ci (1,310-cc) side-valve, limited production V-twin known as the Altoona Engine (named after a famous board track in Altoona, Pennsylvania), producing approximately 40 horsepower. This example was restored by the late Earl Bentley and donated to the Motorcycle Hall of Fame Museum. Similar machines were campaigned at national championship hillclimbs into the 1960s, long after Indian had ceased production. The legendary climber Howard Mitzel, who campaigned Indians over a 40-year career, won AMA championships in 1936, 1939, 1949, 1952, and 1953.*

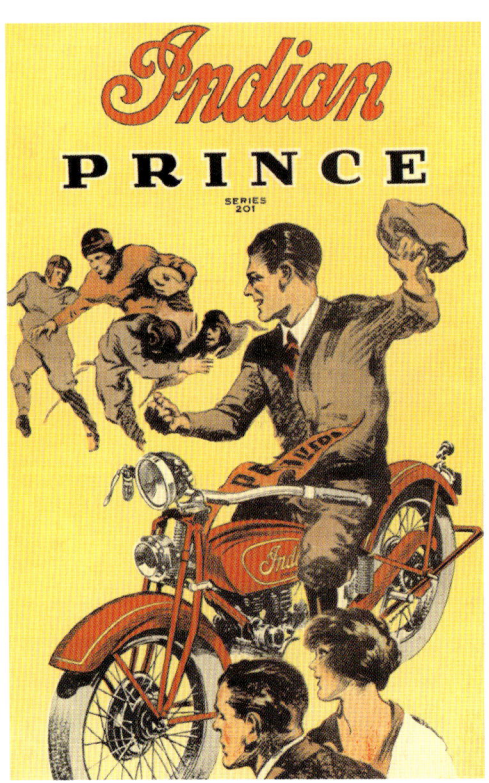

forgot that the Wigwam was intended to be a motorcycle factory. Rather, they saw it as a large-capacity manufacturing facility capable of assembling a wide range of products. Over time, these included automobile shock absorbers, automobile air-circulation devices, and boat motors, almost all of which were ill-fated and unprofitable ventures. Lacking focus on the motorcycle business, Indian leadership eschewed the company's tradition of technical innovation and began to reduce the quality of the product in an effort to reduce manufacturing costs. Creativity, quality, and customer service took a back seat to shareholder value and the bottom line. But as attention to good business continued to decline, so did the bottom line. It was not a good time in history for poor management, because as the industrialized world edged toward world war, Indian found itself—along with other motorcycle companies—facing awesome competition in a hostile operating environment.

Indian's ultimate competitor during the era was not Harley-Davidson, or any motorcycle brand, for that matter. It was the automobile, and specifically the Ford. In 1913, Henry Ford implemented the moving assembly line to speed up and reduce the cost of mass production. He also initiated an installment credit program, enabling many more of the American working class to buy automobiles. Furthermore, in 1914, he doubled the wages of Ford workers from $2.50 to $5.00 per day, placing additional competitive pressure on less-profitable or well-financed companies in the motor vehicle industry. Prior to these initiatives the motorcycle had been the transportation of choice for the masses. Thereafter the motorcycle had no chance of competing against the automobile, which was seen as more practical and easier to operate. As witnessed by Indian's production numbers, motorcycle sales began to level off as automobile sales began to escalate. While Indian and others experienced a flat market for the first time, automobile sales increased by 30 percent. As Ford gained production efficiency, the price of cars began to fall, and soon the Model T's price was on par with that of a motorcycle.

Although Indian's sales continued to grow through 1913, there are indications that the company was feeling the competitive pressure as early as 1912, when it circulated a flyer bearing the headline "Revolutionary Announcement." This revolutionary announcement was that the 1911 $225 price of the four-horsepower single would be reduced to $200, and the seven-horsepower twin would be reduced in price from $300 to $250. Had Indian's demand remained ahead of production, there would have been no justification for price cuts of 11 to 16 percent. As an outgrowth of the popularity of the safety bicycle, motorcycling had become the common man's transportation of choice. But this position was already being displaced by the automobile. Seeking to cling to its traditional market, Indian's "Revolutionary Announcement" brochure declared, "It is to be the motorcycle of the people, and for the people—for all people, and for all classes." How quickly had Indian's fortunes reversed: From posters predicting vastly expanding sales in 1911 to 1912 advertising brochures announcing price cuts!

By the close of the decade, the hundreds of motorcycle brands that had appeared in the American market place were almost all gone, while the ubiquitous Ford was approaching 50 percent of the automobile market share worldwide! But the innovations of Henry Ford were not the only factors that soured the business climate of the motorcycle industry. In the short term, the war seemed to be good for Indian's business, in that military orders helped keep production at about 20,000 units per year, thus stopping further erosion in sales. Following the war, Indian proudly announced that it had met 60 percent of America's military motorcycle requirements. In the long term, however, the political and economic results of World War I were disastrous for Indian and the whole of the motorcycle industry.

Prior to the war, Indian's export market had become as large as half its annual production, and Harley-Davidson's had reached 40 percent. The political and economic fallout of a war that devastated practically every nation in Europe was the application of stiff tariffs by European governments against imported goods—a policy aimed at rebuilding domestic industry. Indian's and Harley's lucrative export markets collapsed almost without warning, practically overnight.

Following a precipitous decline in production numbers at the end of the war, Indian sales and those of its competitors continued to decline throughout the 1920s, as the industrialized world limped toward outright economic collapse and worldwide depression. At the close of the decade, only three American motorcycle manufacturers remained viable: Indian, Harley-Davidson, and Schwinn, which manufactured the Excelsior and Henderson brands.

To compound the distressful operating environment of the motorcycle industry, at the war's end the United States effectively had no governing body for the motorcycle sport. The FAM, founded in 1903, had never become well organized or adequately funded, and it simply was not available to resume the control of competition events after World War I. The FAM still existed on paper, but on a practical basis it was inoperative. By 1920, the Motorcycle and Allied Trades Association—of which Indian and Harley-Davidson were the key players—assumed leadership over the racing scene in the United States, but for the most part, international involvement simply ceased.

With no commercial markets in Europe, it became pointless for Indian to campaign at the Isle of Man or Brooklands . . . or anyplace else. The United States dropped out of the FICM, embarking

## INDIAN PRINCE

*Even after the unenthusiastic responses to the Featherweight and the Model O, Indian continued to try to break into an economy market with a small-bore motorcycle. In 1925, Indian again tried with its 350-cc Prince, a four-stroke side-valve single designed by Charles B. Franklin. It produced about six horsepower, could achieve about 60 miles per hour, and delivered 55 miles per gallon. With this motorcycle, Indian also hoped to improve its export sales, which had collapsed following World War I. This 1928 Prince is owned by Rich Dieter.*

on a long policy of isolationism that lasted well into the late 1960s. This behavior was only logical, because the few American brands remaining found it necessary to focus all of their energy and creativity on simply surviving in the domestic market.

Isolationism played itself out in several important ways. For example, the rivalry that had begun to develop between Indian and Harley-Davidson became intense. Like a long-standing and passionate college football rivalry, it generated energy that likely kept the industry alive, and an intense brand loyalty among dealers and riders from both sides. Secondly, it led indirectly to the vast scope and great strength of the modern American Motorcyclist Association, since dealers throughout America became actively involved in supporting racing and forming large motorcycle clubs. Finally, by focusing exclusively on racing at the domestic level, the M&ATA, and subsequently the AMA, helped evolve a novel and unique concept of racing that made the motorcycle sport—a sport that had previously been the exclusive province of the factories and their teams—available to vast numbers of everyday motorcycle owners.

In addition to the problems of competing with an emerging automobile industry and dealing with the political aftermath of war that brought tough times to the whole of the American motorcycle industry, Indian's predicament was exacerbated by poor strategic decisions. Its board saw World War I military sales as a lucrative opportunity and overcommitted to the war effort, at the expense of the domestic civilian market. This was consistent with its attitude that manufacturing—not marketing—was Indian's primary business. Producing thousands of machines for the War Department was seen as an opportunity to enjoy profits without incurring the expense of promotion and marketing that went along with operating in the civilian market. This strategy brought Indian three years of increased production from 1917 through 1919, but left the company poorly positioned to compete after the war. Its dealers were so neglected and starved for product during the war years that many went broke. Others defected either out of disgust or out of desperation to Harley-Davidson. Some students of American motorcycle history believe that Indian's war-production strategy marked the turning point in its competition with Harley-Davidson. With Indian, success had come early, and the Wigwam had never been required to court and cultivate its dealers. Harley-Davidson had always been playing catch-up against Indian, which some believe gave Harley a greater appreciation for the vital importance of its dealer network.

## A New Engineering Regime

Following Oscar Hedstrom's retirement in 1913, a new engineering regime began the development of a second-generation engine. This included the father-son team of Charles Gustafson, Sr. and Jr., and eventually the great Indian racer Charles B. Franklin, who emigrated from Ireland to America in December of 1916. Gustafson Sr., born in Minnesota in 1869, entered the motorcycle industry in 1906 with Reading-Standard, where he converted a De Dion–type engine to a design with mechanically activated intake valves. He joined Indian as Oscar Hedstrom's assistant in 1907, and a few years thereafter, his son joined the Indian engineering department as well.

The Hedstrom engine—modeled after the De Dion—was a four-stroke F-head design with its intake valve pointing downward, right above its upward-pointing exhaust valve. Both sat in a pocket off the side of the combustion chamber. If one were to draw horizontal lines across the faces of the two valves, extended to a vertical line representing the stroke of the piston, the result would be a Letter "F," thus the descriptive term "F-head." This design is also sometimes called an IOE configuration, meaning "intake over exhaust." It was

**LOOKING FOR "EVERYMAN"**

*George Hendee's runaway success in Indian's early years was based on his idea of creating a motorized vehicle for the masses. With the public mania for the new "safety bicycle," and Oscar Hedstrom's reliable engine, he found a successful combination in a friendly vehicle that weighed less than 100 pounds. As the motorcycle market turned downward, Indian tried time and again to duplicate that success, reasoning that the public would again take to the right kind of lightweight vehicle. Indian tried with the Featherweight, the Model O, and the Prince, but they never again replicated their early success. Pictured is a brochure for the 1925 Indian Prince.*

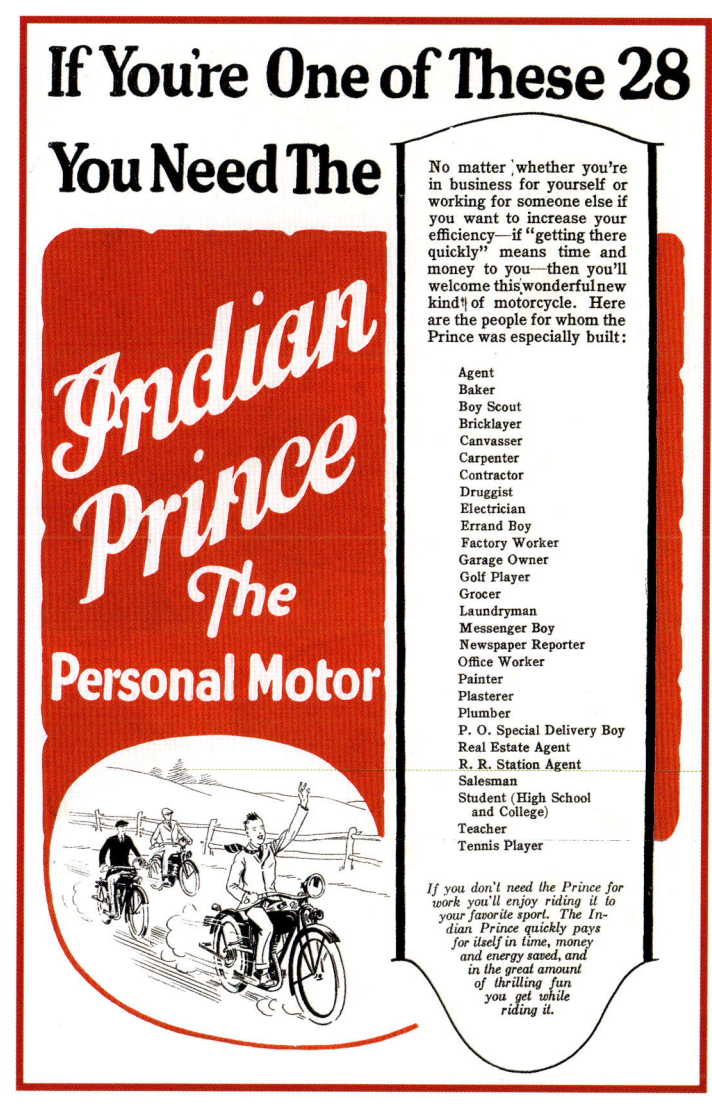

### THE UPSIDE DOWN FOUR

In 1936 and 1937, Indian produced its notorious Upside Down Four, designed by Briggs Weaver. With this machine, the positions of the exhaust and intake valves were reversed, placing the exhaust manifold high on the side of the cylinder head, with the carburetor and intake manifold below. Although Indian hoped to achieve better cooling and combustion efficiency with this configuration, it was considered impractical and ugly by Indian customers. The layout placed the hot exhaust manifold near the rider's right leg, requiring the attachment of a heat shield, which was detrimental to its styling. The first 1936 models, produced in the summer of 1935, had a small chrome-plated heat shield, as on the black and maroon model pictured. This, however, proved insufficient, and a large, unattractive square metal cover was installed to protect the rider's leg, as on the red model shown. In 1937 the bike was given twin carburetors. The Upside Down Four was manufactured for only two years, after which Indian returned to a more conventional design. The 1937 twin-carb model pictured is owned by Guy Jones. The maroon-and-black version, with a single carb and less obtrusive heat shield, is a 1936 model owned by Berland Sullivan. Both have appeared previously at the Motorcycle Hall of Fame Museum.

a simple design, in that only the exhaust valve required mechanical activation, operated by a push rod and driven by a single cam geared to the crankshaft. The intake valve was held in its seat with a spring, and was simply sucked open, bringing in a charge of fuel-air mixture as the piston went downward between the exhaust stroke and the compression stroke. This type of "atmospheric valve" resulted in fewer moving parts, which was an asset at a time when metallurgy was in its relative infancy. But it was not a very efficient engine, compared to subsequent designs.

The Gustafsons had been developing a new side-valve configuration. In the typical side valve, both valves still sit in a pocket off the side of the combustion chamber, but intake and exhaust valves sit side-by-side rather than over and under. And the intake valve—just like the exhaust valve—is activated by a cam driven off the crankshaft. With a cam-activated intake valve, both intake and exhaust can be more precisely controlled and coordinated in timing and duration, resulting in improved efficiency and more power output. Furthermore, the design lends itself to simpler cylinder-head casting and thus lower machining and production costs. Gustafson, who fell historically between Oscar Hedstrom—the Great Medicine Man—and Charles Franklin, who has been revered for his ability to develop high performance side-valve engines, is sometimes overlooked as an important engineering influence. However, his designs made a significant contribution to the evolution of the Indian motorcycle.

A new side-valve engine called the Powerplus appeared in the Indian's line in 1916, in a 61-ci capacity. In the case of the Powerplus, some compromises had been made in valve timing for the sake of simplicity, and all four valves were activated by a single cam with two lobes. Still, it lived up to its name in comparison to the Hedstrom engine it replaced, and it was cheaper to manufacture. Furthermore, by this time carburetion was no longer a mystery, and the Hedstrom carburetor was replaced by a less-expensive unit supplied by Schebler.

Reacting to the tougher sales environment brought on by cheap automobiles, in 1916 Indian also tried to enter an economy market with the Featherweight, a 221-cc (less than 15-ci) two-cycle powered machine with a cartridge-spring fork and no rear suspension. Sales of the Featherweight were disappointing and it was not continued in 1917. As an alternative, Indian tried to attack the economy market with the Model O, a far more sophisticated 257-cc four-stroke, side-valve boxer twin, similar to the British Douglas motorcycle engine. The boxer configuration places the cylinders on opposite sides of the crankshaft. In the case of the Model O, the engine was mounted longitudinally in the frame, with one cylinder pointing forward and one backward. Otherwise, the chassis and running gear were much like that of the 1916 Featherweight. The unfortunate model designation enabled Harley partisans to deride the Model O as the "Model Nothing." Like the Featherweight, it got a disappointing reception in the marketplace, and though suspension improvements were added, it disappeared from the line after 1919.

With a Powerplus single and a Powerplus twin already in the line, in 1920 the new 600-cc (37-ci) Scout appeared. It was designed by Charles B. Franklin, who—as a skilled and experienced championship racer—attacked motorcycle design as a whole package, including engine and chassis. The Scout was a side-valve twin with its gearbox bolted to the engine case, resulting in a semi-unit-construction that offered strength and reliability. Unlike the Powerplus, it had twin cams. Rather than the customary troublesome primary drive chain, the Scout featured an all-gear primary drive bathed in oil. It had a double-loop cradle frame that delivered handling unmatched by any other motorcycle of its era. Of all of the motorcycles Indian ever produced, perhaps the 101 Scout, introduced in 1928 with a 3-inch longer wheelbase and a 1-inch lower saddle, created more die-hard fans devoted to the Indian marque.

The 101 Scout, with its low-weight, responsive engine, and good-handling chassis, was good both on and off the road by contemporary standards. Writing for *Cycle World* magazine in 1967, Thomas Firth Jones said of the Scout, "One of the best afternoons of my life was spent roaring across pastures and through shallow water at the edge of the Chesapeake Bay, while a pack of Indian Chiefs and Harley 74s floundered in my wake." A success from the day it was introduced, Franklin's Scout became the seminal influence over Indian engines for the next 35 years. It was enlarged from 37 to 61 ci in 1922 to become the Chief, and again in 1923 to 74 ci

**THE INDIAN ARROW AT BONNEVILLE**
*Pilot Freddie Ludlow prepares to be bolted into the shell of the Indian Arrow streamliner at Bonneville, 1938. Once fitted into the two halves of the shell, Ludlow had no way of getting out in the event of a crisis.* Photo courtesy of the Motorcycle Hall of Fame Museum Archives, Earl Bentley collection.

to become the Big Chief, the flagship of Indian's touring line. The Powerplus, which was by this time renamed the Standard, was dropped from the line in 1924. The Scout appeared as a 45-ci version in 1927 and was given the name of Police Special. The original 37-ci Scout continued in the line until 1931.

Franklin's Scout continues to achieve success in racing even in the present day. Modified for racing, the Scout defeated more sophisticated designs and carried Indian riders to AMA championships into the 1950s and beyond. As recently as November 2000, a 1934 unstreamlined Scout owned by Jeff Glasserow and ridden by Rusty Lowry set a new A/Vintage Gas Class world land speed record of 127.439 miles per hour.

Following World War I, the big three brands—Indian, Harley, and Excelsior—returned to racing. With America no longer officially involved at the international level, and the industry struggling, motorcycle racing found itself in a state of transition. It became hard to justify expensive factory racing programs and the development of prototype racers in the declining domestic market. Some in the M&ATA wanted to see the big 61-ci (1,000-cc) Class A engines abandoned in favor of the 30.50 (500-cc) machines, arguably because less power would result in safer racing.

There was also concern about how the races were being officiated. While Indian and Harley-Davidson were fierce competitors at many levels, on the political level they could often agree. Addressing the uncertain state of racing under the auspices of a trade association, they decided—along with the other members of the M&ATA—that a new organization was needed to focus strictly on racing. Thus in 1924 they established the American Motorcycle Association, later renamed the American Motorcyc*list* Association.

Distress in the commercial market led to a decision in 1926 that may have been the first step toward making American racing unique, separating it from the traditional international standards that were based on 500-cc and 1,000-cc works machines. Excelsior, which had a lot riding on its Super X, a 45-ci (750-cc) street machine, appealed for and was given a 45-ci championship racing class. However, to provide an adequate field and competition among brands, 30.50-ci engines were allowed to run in the class. In fact, the first national title race for 45-ci machines was won by Jim Davis aboard a 30.50-ci Indian. This rule book compromise represented a practical and democratic attitude toward racing that would come into its own a decade later. Specifically, the attitude of the new AMA was: "The more the merrier." Rather than perpetuate racing as an exclusive high-tech showplace for the best-funded factory, the AMA espoused policies that envisioned racing as an activity directly related to the commercial market. Its willingness to yield to Excelsior's appeal to race its serial-production-based 45, and to allow a mixed formula of 30.50s racing with 45s, was a totally new way of thinking about the motorcycle sport.

But little seemed to stimulate the commercial market, and in both 1923 and 1925, Indian announced price reductions in an attempt to improve motorcycle sales. Although it had produced over a quarter-million motorcycles since 1901, the years when demand outstripped supply had long since passed. In 1925, Indian tried again

**THE ARROW UNDER CONSTRUCTION**
*Pete Andresen works on the skeleton of Hap Alzina's extraordinary Indian Arrow streamliner, circa 1936. Using aircraft technology of the day, the shell was constructed of balsa wood and aircraft spruce, then covered with painted aircraft fabric. Photo courtesy of the Motorcycle Hall of Fame Museum Archives, Earl Bentley collection.*

to penetrate the economy market by introducing the 21-ci single-cylinder, side-valve Prince. This motorcycle, along with the Harley-Davidson "Peashooter," became the basis for a new 21-ci (350-cc) racing class.

By late in the decade, Indian's sales had eroded to less than 5,000 units a year. But rather than focus on its core business, Indian management continued to dissipate the company's declining resources. Money was invested in manufacturing and marketing refrigerators in 1928, but production was never begun. Indian President Louis E. Bauer purchased an automobile shock-absorber patent and plunged the company deeply into manufacturing, distributing, and selling aftermarket shock absorbers. The project was a loser. Furthermore, more than $50,000 was invested in the design of an economy automobile, the brainstorm of President Bauer's son Jack. But the product never came to market. In 1929, Indian bought the Hartford Outboard Motor Company and began to produce Indian boat motors. This too was characteristically unprofitable and further reduced the capital position of the company. As a result, during 1928 and 1929, the company reduced its capital position by $1,250,000 from losses incurred through manufacturing ventures unrelated to motorcycling.

As for its motorcycle business, in 1928 Indian implemented a policy of no longer announcing annual model changes. Rather, changes in the product line were introduced as the company saw fit, and not necessarily tied to a model year. This marketing strategy seemed bizarre and confusing in an industry where big model year announcements had been customary and important, and it did not play well with dealers and customers. Rather than a sound marketing strategy, it more likely represented a convenient and undisciplined approach to product development and manufacturing.

One bright spot in the period that greatly enhanced the Indian image during the following decade was the acquisition of the Ace motorcycle in 1927. Ace was a beautiful four-cylinder machine that had descended from the mighty Henderson Four. After introducing his legendary four-cylinder design in 1912, William Henderson sold his company and design rights to Ignaz Schwinn in 1917. Schwinn/Excelsior continued to build and market the Henderson motorcycle, but William Henderson soon left Schwinn to create another four-cylinder brand called the Ace. Ace developed a sound reputation by setting speed records, but was never a strong company financially. Henderson was killed testing one of his machines on the road in 1922. His associate, engineer Arthur Lemon, continued with the struggling company, which was eventually sold to Michigan Motors and later acquired by Indian. After a transition year in 1928 when the bike was marketed as an Indian Ace, in 1929 it became the Indian Four, embarking on a design and styling evolution that eventually resulted in what many consider one of the most beautiful motorcycles of all time.

A difficult decade ended miserably when, in 1929, the stock market crashed and the world sank into economic depression. Priced out of European markets and beaten at home by the automobile industry, the American motorcycle industry faced an uncertain future. In 1931, Ignaz Schwinn decided that his company would henceforth produce

**PREPARING THE ARROW**
*Mechanic Red Fenwick prepares the Indian Arrow streamliner for a record run. Although Freddie Ludlow set two land speed records, both were aboard the unstreamlined motorcycle. At high speeds, the Indian Arrow became unmanageable, which proved to be the case with many early attempts at streamlining.*
*Photo courtesy of the Motorcycle Hall of Fame Museum Archives, Earl Bentley collection.*

only bicycles, reducing the domestic industry to only two brands: Indian and Harley-Davidson. After World War I, Indian's management had squandered its once-dominant position, although it still produced what many believe was a superior product. Indian now sold half as many motorcycles as Harley-Davidson, which had built its production up to over 10,000 units per year. Charles B. Franklin, who had maintained Indian's technological edge with his side-valve Scout and Chief engines, left the company due to poor health in 1930 and died two years later at the age of 46.

# The du Pont Era

Based on a study of the motorcycle market and the production potential of the Wigwam, financier and industrialist E. Paul du Pont and his brother Francis bought large blocks of Indian stock and sold a controlling interest in the Du Pont Motor Company to Indian in 1929. Both E. Paul and Francis were given seats on Indian's board, and E. Paul was named chairman of its executive committee. The du Ponts, of Wilmington,

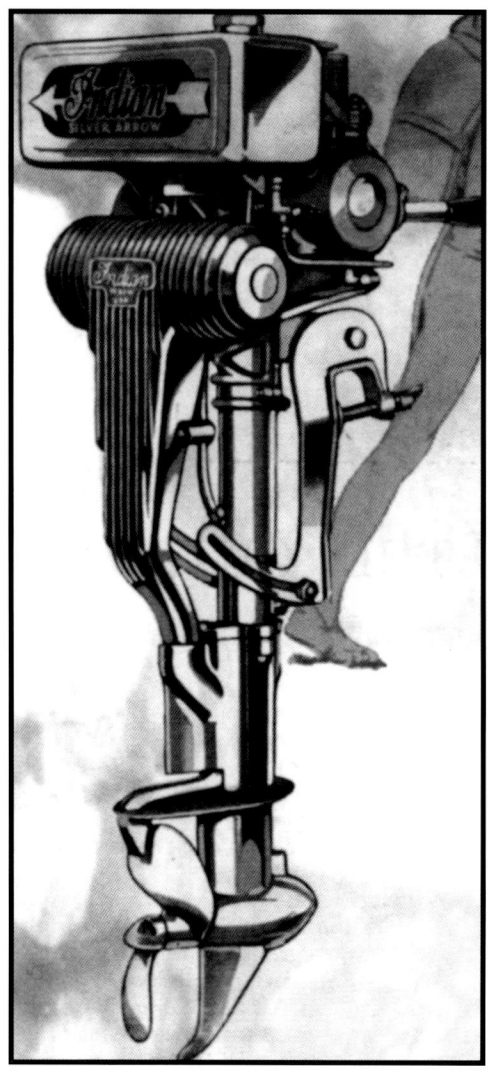

**THE AQUATIC INDIAN**

*Casting about to find manufacturing tasks that could profitably exploit the enormous production capacity of the Wigwam, Indian bought the Hartford Outboard Motor Company in 1929. Given the Briggs Weaver styling treatment, Indian's Silver Arrow outboard motors were attractive and had the appearance of high quality. They were the epitome of the stylish industrial design of the era with a finned muffler integrally cast into the alloy body of the engine. But, like most of Indian's non-motorcycling ventures, they were unprofitable. Upon taking the helm of Indian in 1930, E. Paul du Pont got the company out of the boat motor business posthaste.*

Delaware, were well established in American industry, controlling companies involved in munitions, chemicals, and paints. They were significant stockholders in General Motors, and E. Paul was an engineer by education, fascinated with anything mechanical. He had owned an early Hedstrom motorcycle, and assembled his own motorcycle as a boy. In 1916 he formed a company to build marine engines, then created Du Pont Motors, which built a sporting two-seater—what today would be called a sports car. Fewer than 1,000 Du Pont automobiles were ever built, and production was ceased shortly after the du Ponts got involved with Indian, mainly because such a sporting vehicle was not in sync with America's depressed economic climate.

Upon gaining seats on the Indian board, the du Ponts began immediately to examine the company's finances and operations. They discovered not just generally poor management, but that members of the board of directors were possibly guilty of illegal practices involving insider trading and stock manipulation. With this information, du Pont forced Indian's management team out, took control of the company, and brought aboard Loren E. "Joe" Hosley. Hosley, who had been production manager at Du Pont Motors, took steps immediately to reduce overhead and operating expenses, and got the company out of the outboard motor business. Poor quality control had begun to adversely affect Indian's reputation, and Hosley tried to correct these matters. Small but significant design changes were initiated to make the Chief engines run smoother. Major changes were made in the Four, increasing crankshaft main bearings from three to five to improve reliability. Fit and finish were improved throughout the line, and the ill-conceived "no model year" policy was abandoned with the introduction of the 1931 product line. Hosley also sought tenants to occupy portions of the underutilized Wigwam, and at one point proposed to sell off half the factory.

Although Indian slipped behind Harley-Davidson in terms of engineering during the du Pont era, it leaped ahead in terms of beauty and style, evolving toward the classic design that most people think of today when the name "Indian" is mentioned. Utilizing his family connection with Du Pont Paint, E. Paul began to offer Indians in a wide range of colors. Two-tone designs appeared, and in some model years as many as 24 different combinations of paint were available as standard offerings. Furthermore, for only $5, a customer could order his Indian with any nonstandard color available in the Du Pont line of automotive enamels.

In 1932, a "saddle" gas tank brought a new and modern look, and in 1934, beautifully rounded and valanced fenders were introduced on the Sport Scout. A year later these fenders were included on all models. Styled by Briggs Weaver, they were the precursors of the famous full-skirted fenders that appeared in 1940.

But not all changes went in the right direction. Indian was a company in trouble, and while emphasis was placed on the style and appearance of the product, many substantive changes were aimed strictly at saving money and reducing manufacturing costs. One such change was the replacement of the fabulous 101 Scout with the 203 Scout, known as the Standard Scout, in 1932. The Standard Scout was nothing but a Scout engine in a Chief frame. One of Indian's greatest motorcycles had been replaced with an inferior product for the sake of standardizing and reducing the cost of production. While internal changes were made to produce smoother and more powerful engines, nothing was done to fundamentally update the Franklin side-valve design. In the meantime, in the throes of the Depression, Harley-Davidson invested heavily in an engineering project that resulted in the legendary 61-ci Model EL, which became affectionately known as the Knucklehead. This engine, plus Harley-Davidson's decision to mass produce a racing engine in the WR, moved the Motor Company even further ahead of Indian.

In spite of du Pont's financial acumen and Hosley's production expertise, Indian continued to suffer within the poor economy and a declining market. By 1933 the Wigwam was running at only 5 percent production capacity, and sales slipped to under 1,700 units. Indian had produced nearly twice as many motorcycles in 1907, its fifth year in the business. Harley-Davidson sales were down as well, but still consistently doubled those of Indian. Toward the end of the decade, Indian stock—for which du Pont had paid $11.75 in 1930—was down to $2.50 per share.

During the 1930s, Indian and Harley came together again under the auspices of the AMA to take American motorcycle racing in a unique and unusual direction. Previously, racing had been staged to showcase the engineering prowess of the factories and the skill of factory riders, and as entertainment for the public. It had been conceived as advertising to sell more motorcycles to more people. But in the Depression years, fewer people were interested in or capable of buying motorcycles, and after the advent of inexpensive automobiles, no one really needed a motorcycle. Motorcycling had become an enthusiast activity for a relatively small segment of the population. It became clear that the only likelihood for the survival of a declining industry was to provide opportunities for these enthusiasts to enjoy their motorcycles, wear them out, and hopefully buy more. Thus, it was concluded that racing should not be the province of a few factory stars and a handful of works machines. It should become the playground of anyone who owned a motorcycle.

This marketing strategy took the form of a new set of racing rules called Class C racing, introduced in 1932. Unlike the previous A and B racing classes for 1,000-cc and 500-cc purpose-built works machines, the new Class C class provided racing for serial production motorcycles. The machines had to have stock engines and chassis from motorcycles available through any motorcycle dealer, and the rules provided for very few modifications.

Class C racing may have come about in part because of the vision of Indian advertising department employee Ted Hodgdon, who traveled to Somers, New York, in April 1931 to see a new event being staged by the Crotona Motorcycle Club. With the idea

of conducting a miniature British Tourist Trophy, the club had carved a meandering racetrack through an apple orchard and over a hill. Because this kind of course was entirely unsuitable for powerful and fragile works track racing machines, the competitors that day were riding street production motorcycles. Hodgdon immediately recognized the sales and marketing potential for this new kind of American TT racing, and he returned to Springfield to convince Joe Hosley and AMA President Jim Wright that this idea needed to be sold to other clubs throughout the nation. Wright agreed to publish TT rules in the 1931 AMA rule book, including a diagram of a TT course sketched out by Hodgdon.

As with any novel and radical idea, Class C racing was ridiculed in the beginning. It was seen as bush-league and amateurish. Of course, in a very real sense, that's what it was supposed to be. It was supposed to take racing to the masses, and to create opportunities to race at the grassroots level. But both Indian and Harley-Davidson were behind the idea because neither company could afford any longer to fund big racing departments, build expensive prototype racers, and sponsor factory teams.

Although it departed radically from all motorcycle racing tradition on both national and international levels, Class C racing was the right idea for its time. It caught on to the extent that in 1934 the AMA took the bold step of announcing that national championship points would no longer be awarded for Class A or Class B meets. Henceforth, all national championship meets would be run under Class C rules. In fact, some Class A championships were staged as late as 1939 for works 30.50 singles, but for all practical purposes, Class A racing in America was dead. Large fields of competitors began to turn out at championship events

### 1939 WORLD'S FAIR FOUR

*After E. Paul du Pont took control of Indian in 1930, he brought aboard as head designer Briggs Weaver, who had been a body designer for sporting two-seat Du Pont automobiles. In 1934, Weaver executed a styling treatment on the Sport Scout that was so popular it was applied to the whole model line in 1935. This treatment include a well-shaped saddle tank, originally introduced in 1932, and beautifully rounded and valanced fenders. Later, in 1940, Weaver produced the radical full-skirted fender for which Indian has become famous. However, it was controversial in its day, and many still believe the 1938 and 1939 Indian Fours to be some of the most beautiful motorcycles ever created. With their long engine, curvaceous bodywork, and two-tone color schemes, they stand out as examples of industrial art, as America entered the streamlined era of style and design. The 1939 Four pictured is a special World's Fair commemorative model, painted in official World's Fair colors. This original, unrestored example is owned by Leon Blackman, and appeared previously at the Motorcycle Hall of Fame Museum.*

**1939 TRAFFIC CAR**

*During the 1930s, Indian estimated that about 40 percent of its sales were for police or utilitarian use. To provide a delivery van for small businesses, Indian produced the special order Traffic Car, built on a three-wheeled chassis. The vehicle pictured—a 1939 Traffic Car with a 74-ci Chief engine—may be the only surviving example of these limited production vehicles. The body was built for Indian by the Waterhouse Company of Webster, Massachusetts. It is owned by the Motorcycle Hall of Fame Museum.*

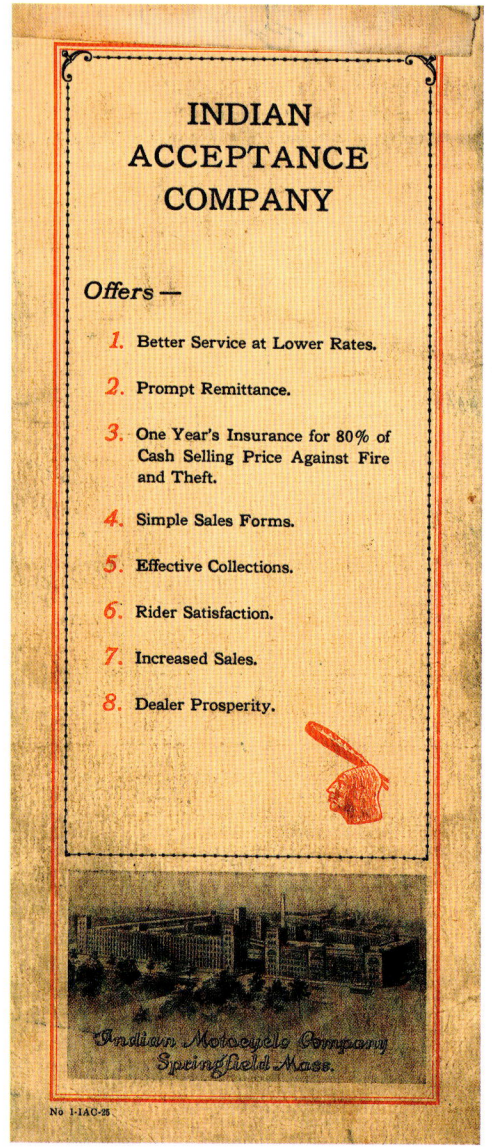

because, with racing motorcycles readily available through any Indian or Harley-Davidson dealership, victory was determined strictly by one's skill in the saddle. Class C was the democratizing of motorcycle racing in America.

Hillclimbing had become more popular during the 1920s, and gained even more popularity during the Depression, in part because hillclimbs were less expensive to promote and organize. During this era all three leading factories—including Excelsior until 1930—continued to sponsor teams and build special hillclimbing machines. However, these efforts were far less costly than the factory racing programs during the heyday of Class A racing.

The strategy of selling motorcycles through sporting activity, and the extent to which Indian supported this movement, is revealed in a letter from Indian Vice President and General Manager Loren Hosley to Indian dealers, dated March 1, 1934. Hosley wrote:

> *"About 60 percent of the motorcycle business is so-called 'sport,' and the balance is police and commercial. Realizing this, the factories looked for a method to help our dealers with this 'sport business.' Many ways have been tried but to have a centralized association which could promote and help general motorcycle sport has proved the best and most effective means, rather than for each factory to handle this promotion by itself. Therefore, both motorcycle factories decided to put all their support and effort into the AMA, with the idea that we could give the greatest help to our dealers in this manner.*
>
> *"I am asking you to join [the AMA] for no other reason than to help you in your business. Your activity in the AMA will be directly reflected in dollars by the 'sport business' you will create."*

Indian's sport-based marketing strategy was well timed with its product development, because in 1934 the Sport Scout appeared. This motorcycle enabled Indian to excel in the new Class C racing program. The Scout became the basis for racing motorcycles that were able to beat Harley-Davidsons into the 1950s, long after Indian had ceased production of the Sport Scouts. The Sport Scout has been credited to design chief G. Briggs Weaver, but a young member of the engineering staff named Jimmy Hill had a significant hand in its design. Like Charles Franklin, who had designed the original Scout, Hill was an able competition rider and brought both formal engineering training and personal motorcycling experience and enthusiasm to his task.

Two events significant to the future of Indian occurred in 1940. Production Manager Joe Hosley died in February, which likely affected the extent to which E. Paul du Pont was willing to continue his struggle to improve the fortunes of the Wigwam. And that same year, Indian initiated a radical styling departure, introducing the full-skirted fenders that have become the aesthetic trademark of the brand. Along with the large and graceful fenders came a well-shaped fuel tank and a large, curving chain guard. Even the finning on the cylinders and heads of the side-valve engine were shaped to enhance the new

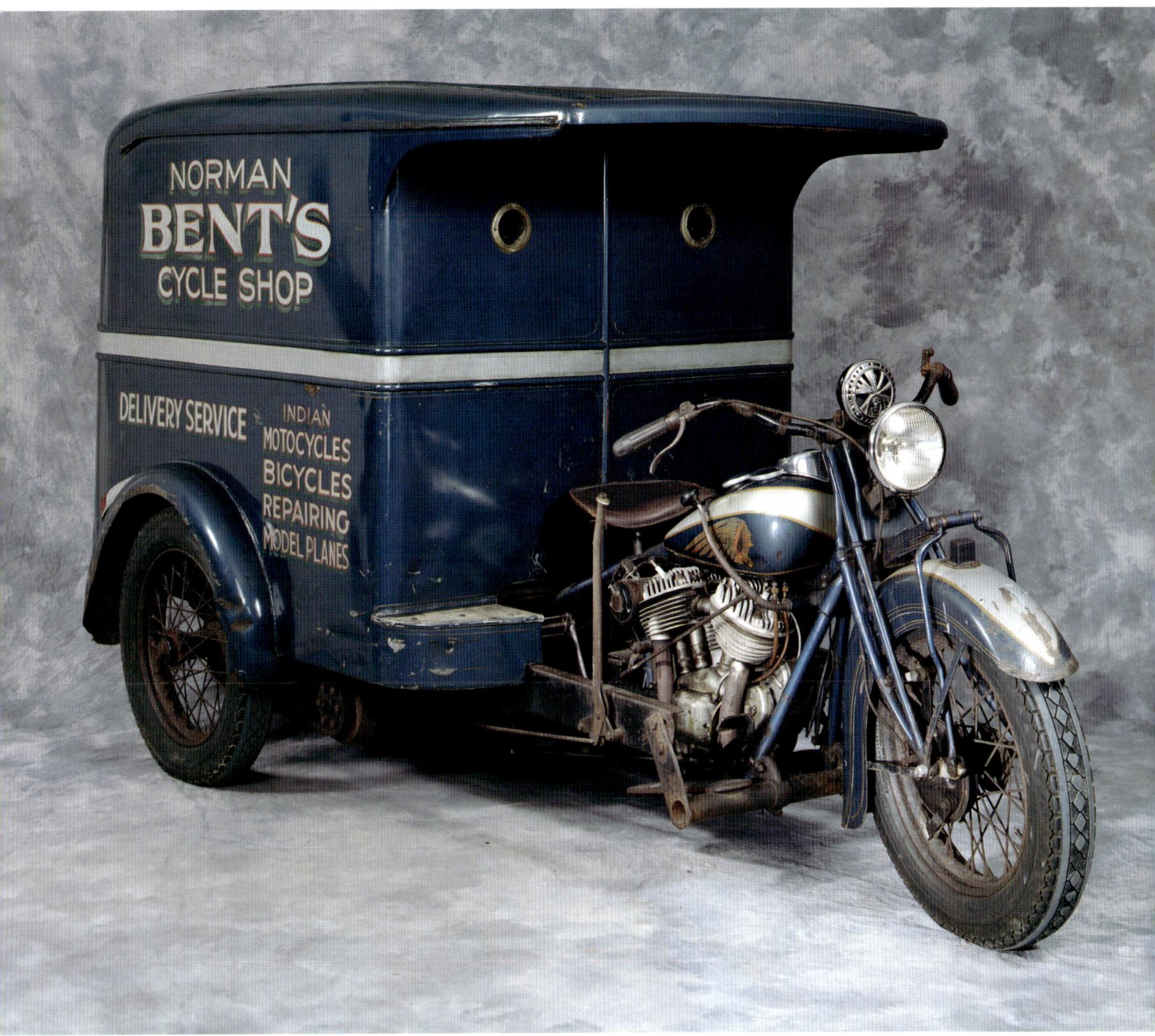

### INDIAN'S SKIRTED SENSATION

**Announcing its 1940 product line, the October-November 1939 issue of Indian News declares, "New 1940 Indian Creates Sensation." The new full-skirted Indian was like nothing that had come before it. Its styling cues came from the American design trend know as "streamlining." This trend had been evident in American industrial design since the mid-1930s, and had appeared on such famous automobiles as the Auburn and the Cord, designed by Gordon Buehrig, and the locomotives of Raymond Loewy. The treatment was controversial when it was introduced, but over time became the stylistic signature of Indian motorcycles. Although it represented less than 15 years of Indian's long history, it defined the Indian that people remember.**

streamlined and curvaceous styling. This treatment, conceived by G. Briggs Weaver, was controversial at the time, but heralded by Indian's advertising department as "The style-blazer of a new era of motorcycling."

Weaver had been brought aboard by E. Paul du Pont in 1932, following the death of Charles Franklin. He had previously worked as a car body designer for Du Pont Motors, and likely took his styling cues from some of the more luxurious automobiles of the period. Unlike any motorcycle before it, the front fender of the 1940 Indian dipped forward over the leading edge of the tire, almost like the fender of an Auburn or a Cord. Weaver left Indian in 1943 to join an engineering project with Torque Manufacturing Company in Plainfield, Connecticut, not knowing at the time that this project would figure prominently in Indian's future.

With the military buildup for World War II, the motorcycle industry finally received an economic boost that put an end to an era of uncertainty and depression. By 1942, Indian was producing 10,000 units per year, mostly for military use. Indian produced military models with both 30.50-ci and 45-ci engines, whereas the WLA, Harley-Davidson's basic military model, only came with a 45-ci engine. As a result, Harley-Davidsons were assigned to the U.S. Army, and many were sent on to Russia. Indian's 741 was a favorite with Allied nations, such as Great Britain and Canada, because of their traditional familiarity with the 500-cc engine category. Indian also built gray-painted Chiefs outfitted with sidecar delivery boxes for the U.S. Navy.

An experimental shaft-driven machine called the Model 841 was also built by Indian during this time. It was designed in response to military specifications for a motorcycle to use in North Africa, where the desert sand could quickly destroy a drive chain. Harley-Davidson created the XA, which contained an engine faithfully copied from a 750-cc side-valve military BMW. Indian's response was far more creative. The 841 contained a side-valve 90-degree V-twin, mounted longitudinally in the frame. Fewer than 1,000 841s were ever produced, due in part to a lack of need after the defeat of the Germans in North Africa, and in part because of the advent of the Jeep. As had happened with the advent of the Ford Model T earlier in the century, the motorcycle found itself pushed out of another market niche by an inexpensive, innovative, and enduring four-wheeled vehicle.

With the end of hostilities, Indian cut its work week from 60 to 48 hours. Although production had increased as a result of the war, the military windfall brought no permanent benefits to the company. To the contrary, Indian came out of World War II with now badly outdated technology and a weak dealer network. In spite of a valiant effort to improve the fortunes of the once-proud Indian, E. Paul du Pont managed to only basically break even, recording a net loss of about $250,000 over his entire 15-year regime. In November 1945, the company was sold to an investment group headed up by Ralph B. Rogers, a millionaire industrialist involved in the manufacture of diesel engines, power lawn mowers, air-conditioning equipment, and railway motor cars. Du Pont left behind an Indian with classic styling and a still-strong brand name, but an outdated engine design. The company was ill-positioned to face its future, based on its great tradition alone.

## Indian's Big Gamble

The aftermath of World War II was in many ways the opposite of World War I, when tariffs were erected by the nations of Europe to stave off foreign imports and protect domestic industries. Post–World War I economic policy was based on isolation, not cooperation. Economic policy following World War II was determined by the European Recovery Act of 1947, more commonly known as the Marshall Plan. Named for U.S. Secretary of State George C. Marshall, the Marshall Plan set up the Economic Cooperation Administra-

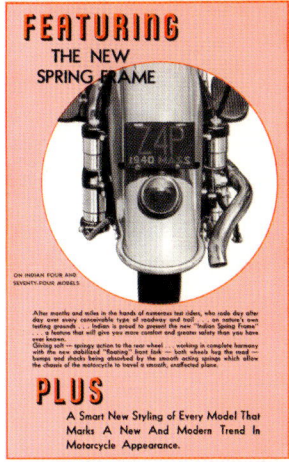

tion, which pumped $12 billion in foreign aid into European economies between 1948 and 1951. Perhaps more important in the long run than the injection of foreign aid was the fact that the Marshall Plan fostered cooperation between European and North American governments in the exchange of goods and technology. It stimulated international markets and caused cross-pollination of important technical ideas.

Every aspect of commerce and the arts was impacted by the Marshall Plan, not the least of these being the motorcycle industry. It resulted in a flood of imported motorcycles from England and Europe. These motorcycles had evolved along different technological lines than those of Indian and Harley-Davidson. They were smaller and lighter and typically had single-cylinder or vertical twin-cylinder engines. They were more agile and better at sporting activity than the big American V-twins. And, based in part on a strong dollar and deflated European currencies, they were affordable. Americans had seen such motorcycles in limited numbers prior to the war. But during the war, American GIs in Europe became more familiar with them, and they liked what they saw. Thus, a strong American postwar economy and a more open-minded attitude toward European ideas and products translated into a strong U.S. market for imported motorcycles.

Suddenly, the isolated domestic marketing environment through which Indian and Harley-Davidson had struggled during the past quarter-century came to an end. Both companies found themselves in an environment in which many more people could afford and wanted to buy motorcycles. But they also found themselves overrun with imported competing brands. Harley-Davidson reacted by continuing to pursue its core business, the big-twin touring market. It introduced a 125-cc two-stroke appropriated

**THE INDIAN WE ALL REMEMBER**
*Designer Briggs Weaver brought Indian into the age of streamlined industrial design typified by Auburn automobile and Hudson-class locomotives. It started with his valanced-fendered designs of the mid-1930s, then reached complete expression with the full-skirted Chief in 1940. In case anyone could fail to notice, this 1940 sales brochure declared Indian the "Style Blazer of a New Era of Motorcycling."*

## 1946 INDIAN CHIEF

***During the 1940s, Indian attracted customers through color and style. No other motorcycle looked like the skirt-fendered Chief, especially when it came in two-tone color schemes. Customers not satisfied with the wide array of standard colors available could special order their Indian in any of the nonstandard automotive colors available in the DuPont Paint catalog. This maroon-and-cream 1946 Chief is owned by Tim Laurent, and appeared previously at the Motorcycle Hall of Fame Museum.***

# Here's the Silver Arrow

A Worthy Brother to the Motorcycle that holds the World's Speed Records—the World's Endurance Records—and other scalps earned in Competition where *Superior Performance Wins!*

HERE it is—the INDIAN Silver Arrow Outboard Motor—with a host of exclusive INDIAN features that make for reliability, long life, and *punch!* An ease of starting heretofore unknown in outboards—and real economy of operation—are further features of this new INDIAN Motor. Note the strong, clean-cut design—and the absence of small parts. An indication of typical INDIAN stamina.

It's a Class B Motor of 19.36 cubic inches piston displacement — most efficient, two-stroke, three port design. It's just loaded with horse-power—starts at a turn of the flywheel and rev's up to 4500 R.P.M. with a smoothness that's a treat to the outboard motor enthusiast. The new INDIAN cylinder design, employing a solid aluminum alloy head—and the new "Full-View" cooling system, helps this motor to deliver maximum performance when you want it.

This new INDIAN motor is designed and built throughout to the INDIAN standard of quality and wherever possible, especially in some of the larger parts, high grade aluminum alloy is used, with the result that the motor weighs only 68 pounds.

Silence is the key-note of the Silver Arrow Motor. The new INDIAN cast aluminum silencer, made in *one piece* carries the exhaust under water with a minimum of back-pressure. This silencer is another carefully engineered feature with its ample cooling fins which help to dissipate heat effectually.

Large oversize bearings, cylinders of best grade cast-iron set in aluminum alloy water jackets, and ball bearings wherever necessary, plus a very thorough system of lubrication, contribute toward the long life in service which one expects of INDIAN products.

You must see—and try—this new INDIAN motor to appreciate outboard motoring at its best.

*Above: Note the clean, compact, design of the Silver Arrow Motor, and the absence of small parts. Simplicity and stamina are built into this design. The spacious muffler, cast in one single piece of aluminum alloy, is well finned for cooling.*

*At Right: A rear view of the INDIAN Silver Arrow Motor showing the carefully streamlined lower housing which slips through the water with minimum resistance. The design of the anti-cavitation plate is such that it facilitates exhaust by suction.*

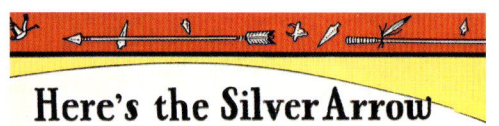

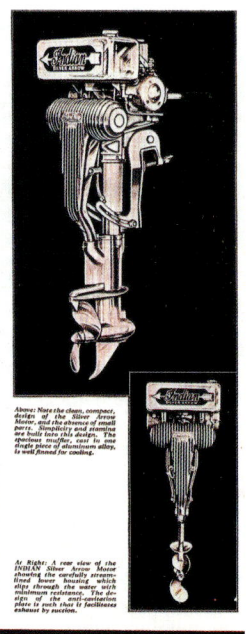

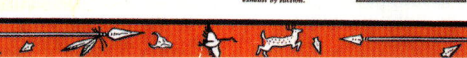

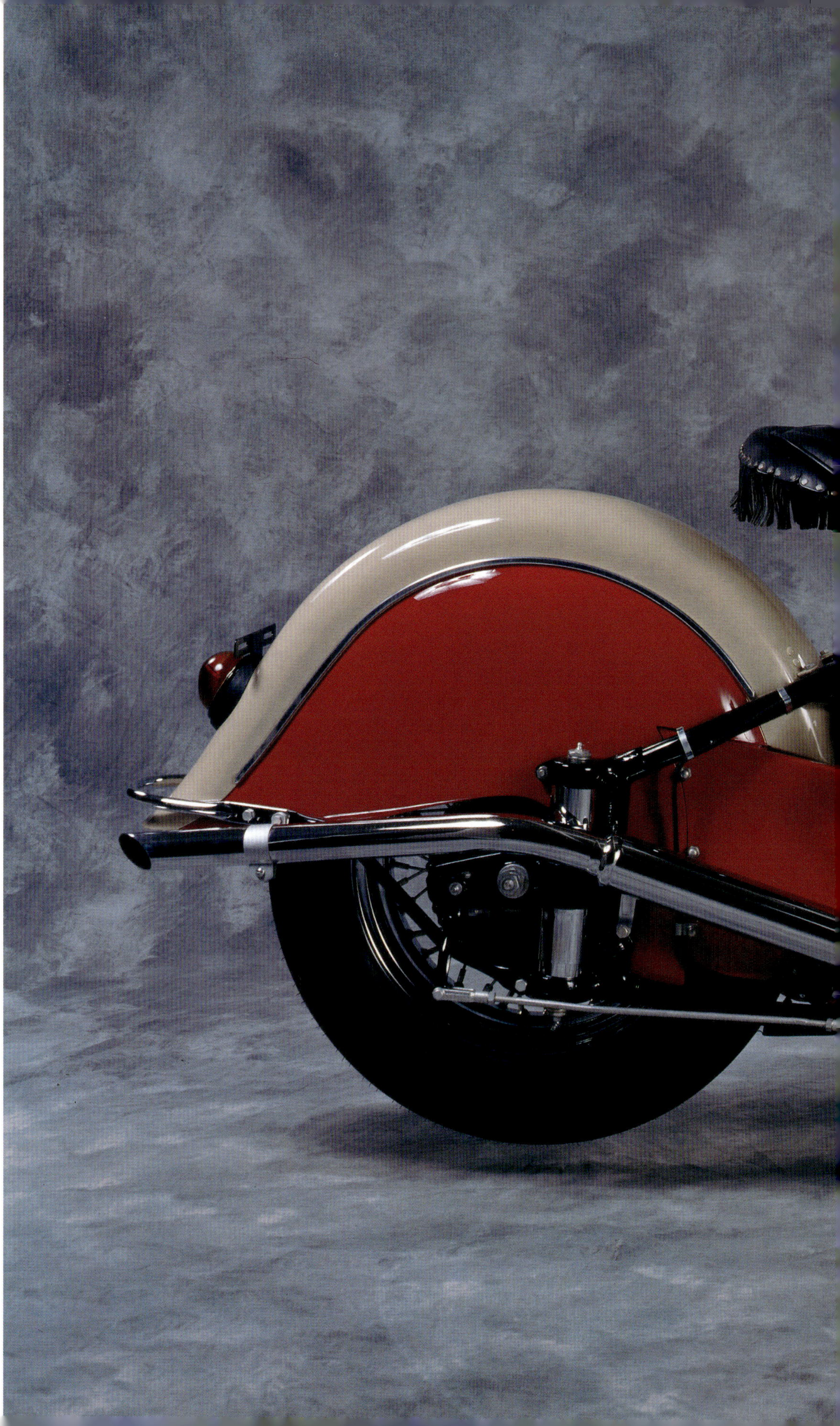

from the German firm DKW, then eventually produced the 750-cc side-valve K Model—followed by the overhead valve XL Sportster—to compete with the quick and agile imports. Indian took a more radical course, betting the whole farm on a strategy to reinvent itself and compete head-to-head in terms of style and technology with the British "lightweights."

Indian had only one model—the 1946 Chief—at the end of the war, and it represented old technology. Harley-Davidson had been marketing overhead valve technology on its big twins for a decade. Additionally, Harley-Davidson had several models in its line and a strong dealer network, and was more than doubling Indian's annual sales. In reaction to Indian's unfavorable position in the market, Ralph Rogers brought to the company a brave and risky vision. He saw young Americans responding to a different style of motorcycling imported from Europe, and he concluded that this would be America's motorcycling future. Rogers believed the market called for a totally new Indian—a product equal in technology and design to the imported vertical twins, and unencumbered by Indian's traditions.

In 1946, Rogers purchased Torque Manufacturing, the same company to which Indian designer Briggs Weaver had gone in 1943 to join an engine development project. Torque had been set up during the war by Belgian emigrants Jean and Paul Stokvis, who fled Europe just before Hitler overran the Benelux countries. It was their intention to develop a motorcycle in the European style, based on an engine design quite reminiscent of the overhead valve designs made famous by British motorcycle engineering patriarch Edward Turner.

Torque espoused a "modular design" concept. The idea was that a whole family of engines could be produced in various sizes, built around the shared parts of a common cylinder, head, and valvetrain design. Based on a 175-cc overhead valve design, the result was similar to the British imports that had invaded America, represented by brands such as Triumph, BSA, Matchless, Royal Enfield, and others. Starting with the basic Torque engine unit, one could theoretically produce a 175-cc single, a 350-cc twin, and an 700-cc four-cylinder, all of which shared many parts and castings. That is exactly what Ralph Rogers set out to do, except that the basic engine was enlarged to 220-cc, leading to a 220-cc single, a 440-cc twin, and an 880-cc four.

A postwar Scout and a new Four based on Indian's traditional engineering were in prototype development when Rogers acquired the company, but they were never completed. Rather, Rogers committed Indian entirely to the new concept. The big, traditional V-twin Chief remained in the model line, but nearly total resources were devoted to the development and introduction of the new generation of overhead-valve Indians. Rogers also saw no advantage in making a clean start at an outdated factory with decrepit machinery, so in 1947 Indian announced that an entirely new motorcycle was on the way, and that it would be built in a new plant in East Springfield. The big Wigwam was put up for sale.

In 1948, Rogers and a team of his executives conducted a multi-city tour to introduce the 220-cc Arrow and the 440-cc Scout, and to talk about Indian's new vision and its new marketing plan. Rogers saw a confident and financially healthy America bursting to travel and pursue new experiences, and he envisioned a market ready for a "gentleman's motorcycle." He saw progressive young fathers riding Indian Scouts, with their sons coming into motorcycling aboard Indian Arrows. He laid out for the dealers a two-pronged marketing strategy: Traditional Indian loyalists would buy the big V-twin Chief, but a whole new generation of gentlemen motorcyclists would clamor for the new-style Indian lightweights. He promised that Indian would support its dealers and this marketing strategy by spending more money on national magazine advertising than any other company in the motorcycle industry. Traditional Indian dealers were skeptical, but

**MILITARY INDIANS**

*Indian produced the Model 640B for military use. It was basically a Scout refitted to Army specifications—the 741, with a 30.50-ci engine (500-cc); and the 841, an all-new shaft drive 90-degree V-twin. The U.S. Army preferred Harley-Davidson's WLA, and most of Indian's production of the Model 741 went to allied forces in Canada and the United Kingdom. The 841 was Indian's answer to Army specifications for a motorcycle that could be used in the hot, dusty conditions of the sands of North Africa. A shaft drive was required because chains and sprockets were chewed up by the abrasive sand. The 841 engine was mounted longitudinally in the frame, like a BMW or Moto Guzzi. Due to the defeat of the Germans in North Africa, not many 841s were ever built. Another factor that adversely affected the production of all military motorcycles was the invention of the military Jeep. The motorcycle pictured is owned by Frank DeGenero, and has appeared previously at the Motorcycle Hall of Fame Museum.*

## SPORT SCOUT DIRT TRACKER

*The Indian Sport Scout was one of the Wigwam's greatest motorcycles. As a road machine, it appeared in 1934 with beautifully flared and valanced fenders, which were included on all models in 1935. The timing of the Sport Scout was especially good since it became a potent and successful competition motorcycle under the AMA's new Class C rules. While its design was credited to Indian design chief Briggs Weaver, racer Jimmy Hill had a big hand in its development. The Sport Scout was tuned to ever-higher states of performance over two decades, and was still earning national championship titles for Indian when the company was sliding into bankruptcy in the mid-1950s. Its late glory days came at the hands of Bobby Hill, Bill Tuman, and Ernie Beckman, known as the Indian Wrecking Crew. Even after this threesome had switched to British motorcycles for AMA road races, they still campaigned Sport Scouts at national championship dirt-track races. Hill earned the AMA Number 1 Plate for Indian with victories at Springfield, Illinois, in 1951 and 1952; Tuman kept the prize for Indian by winning Springfield in 1953. The last AMA championship for Indian came when Beckman won at Williams Grove, Pennsylvania, on October 11, 1953. This motorcycle is Bill Tuman's championship Sport Scout, still owned by Tuman.*

enthusiasm for a vital and growing motorcycle market was running high, and Rogers' tour was a big success. The national dealer roster, which had declined to about 450 dealers during the years of Indian's neglect of its dealer network, doubled as a result of the new-product announcement tour.

Consistent with Rogers' plan to reach a new, upscale middle-American customer, Indian gave away new motorcycles to Hollywood stars and sports heroes. Matinee idol Alan Ladd and football star Johnny Lujak were featured on the cover of *Indian News*, National Broadcasting Company Sports Director Bill Stern was featured aboard his new Arrow in *Mechanix Illustrated,* in a story entitled "How to Ride a Motorcycle," and publicity stills were circulated to the media showing Jane Russell taking delivery of her new Indian. To reinforce the idea that the new Indian lightweight motorcycle was socially acceptable and easy to ride, product photos featured young, wholesome, smiling coeds astride Scouts and Arrows.

In concept, it was a plan that seemed right for the time. But in execution, the new Indian was a disaster. Announced in 1948, the new Arrows and Scouts did not appear until July 1949, and then only in small quantities. By rushing a totally new motorcycle into production at a new manufacturing facility, Indian found itself plagued with production and quality-control problems. Furthermore, the new designs—what Indian coined their "Dyna-Torque" engines—had been inadequately tested prior to serial production. They proved quite unreliable. Cam drive gears were mismatched, bearings were damaged during assembly, improperly spoked wheels and hubs disintegrated in use, and faulty lubrication systems resulted in catastrophic engine failures. Thomas Firth Jones wrote about the motorcycle in *Cycle World* in 1967, "It had a fantastically unreliable magneto ignition system, and a very weak bottom end." Then he added, wryly, "Gentlemen do not like to throw rods."

Some theorize that the project went wrong from the moment the basic Torque unit was pushed beyond its original engineering parameters, from 175 to 220 cc. That, however, probably had less to do with engine failures than did shoddy manufacturing and inadequate testing. Veteran Indian racer and engineer Jimmy Hill tested the Arrow prototype in 1946 and submitted a scathing report, but it was buried by members of middle management, who were more dedicated to telling Ralph Rogers what he wanted to hear. To make matters worse, in order to focus all of its energy on solving its Dyna-Torque engine design and manufacturing problems, Indian discontinued the Chief in 1949. This enraged many loyal, longtime dealers. Some even defected to Harley-Davidson.

The new concept also failed to recognize the traditional role of racing in the American motorcycle industry. When introduced, the new Indians were not suitable for any racing category in the AMA rule book. To address this problem, an already unreliable engine was enlarged from 440 to 500 to create the Laconia Scout, a competition-worthy motorcycle. To assert the new Indian in the arena of championship competition, Rogers entered a team of 12 prototypes at Laconia in 1949, all piloted by paid factory riders. It was a total fiasco with not one Indian finishing the race.

Marketing mistakes and racetrack misfortune aside, the blow from which Indian could not recover came in September 1949, when the British government announced a 25 percent devaluation in the Pound Sterling, reducing its exchange value from approximately $4.00 to approximately $3.00. This devaluation had the theoretical effect of reducing the retail price of British products—including motorcycles—by 25 percent in the American retail market. Retail British motorcycle prices did not in fact decline by a full 25 percent, but they fell enough to hurt Indian. The new Indians, which had been priced to compete head-to-head with British imports, were now conspicuously overpriced. By the end of 1949, the new Indian had established a reputation for unreliability, had embarrassed the brand on the racetrack, lacked the support of the dealer network, and cost more to purchase than imports with a better reputation. Dealer and customer defection continued.

**1948 MODEL 648 "BIG BASE" SCOUT DAYTONA WINNER**

*Indian's Sport Scout was out of production by 1942. With Harley-Davidson pumping WR racing motorcycles into the market, Indian needed something to keep its hand in the game. The Wigwam was focused on building the new lightweight model line, and very little money was available for a racing program. With relatively little investment, the Model 648 Scout was developed. It got its name from a big crankcase with a larger oil sump and the use of Model 841 flywheels from the 90-degree V-twin experimental military model. Only about 50 648 Scout engines were assembled, and exactly how many complete motorcycles is not known. However, Indian got a big payoff with a Daytona 200 victory in 1948, delivered by Floyd Emde at an average speed of 84.10 miles per hour. A well-tuned 648 Scout was capable of 7,000 rpm and 115 miles per hour with road racing gearing. This is the actual Daytona winner, owned by Jim Sutter of Sugar Grove, Illinois. The Daytona 200 was won three times by riders aboard Indians; in addition to Emde in 1948, they were Ed Kretz Sr., at an average speed of 74.10 miles per hour at the inaugural Daytona 200 in 1937, and Johnny Spiegelhoff in 1947, at an average speed of 77.14 miles per hour.*

Hap Alzina, the long-time western states distributor for Indian, was one of the brand's greatest supporters and the Wigwam's greatest assets. He was highly respected by his dealers, and in 1948 was responsible for 20 percent of Indian's total worldwide sales. In Indian's declining years, he sometimes paid for large orders in advance just so the factory could make its payroll. Although Alzina worked as hard as anyone to keep Indian alive, he finally had enough, and in 1949 became an importer for BSA. Many of his dealers went with him. Similarly, Ed "Iron Man" Kretz, whose name had been associated with Indian victories on racetracks all over America, finished his racing career aboard a Triumph and became a Triumph dealer.

## The End of Days

As an American motorcycle manufacturer, Indian never recovered. The Chief was brought back into the line in 1950 and produced with improved suspension, fit, and finish until 1953, but the brand's reputation was hopelessly damaged. Desperate for capital, Rogers made a deal with Englishman John Brockhouse of J. Brockhouse & Company, Ltd. Brockhouse invested $1.5 million, was given a seat on the Indian Motorcycle Company board of directors, and the Indian Sales Company was created. With this company, Brockhouse was allowed to distribute through Indian's dealer network the British brands under his control, including AJS, Douglas, Matchless, Royal Enfield, Norton, and Vincent.

For a company that envisioned its principal business as competing with British brands, it was like inviting the fox into the henhouse, or, shall we say, inviting Custer into the wigwam! Brockhouse set out immediately to use his influence with the board of directors to undermine Rogers. In January 1950, Brockhouse engineered a coup that removed Rogers as CEO. Leftover Arrows and Scouts were sold as 1950 models, the 500-cc Warrior and Warrior TT models were brought into the line, and the Chief was

enlarged to 80 ci. The Warrior TT was a much-improved product with considerable development potential for racing, but by this time the reputation of the vertical twin was tarnished beyond repair.

Few people wanted the new overhead-valve Indians when they could get British bikes that really worked, and the Chief, though more beautiful than ever, was sadly outdated by Harley-Davidson's overhead-valve touring bikes. Production was suspended in 1953. A letter to Indian dealers spoke of a "production holiday" to allow the company to regroup, but the so-called holiday never came to an end. Production never resumed. Indian, which had at one time been the largest and most respected motorcycle manufacturer in the world, was now reduced to a distribution and marketing company for foreign motorcycles.

To American enthusiasts, John Brockhouse became the Great Satan in Indian's End of Days scenario. An article appeared in the April 1954 issue of Cycle Magazine entitled "The Vanishing American." The article was illustrated with a sketch of the famous Laughing Indian logo turned into a weeping Indian. Editorializing on the decision to cease production, publisher Floyd Clymer wrote:

> "In August of 1953, I made a trip to Springfield to learn Indian's 1954 plans first-hand and to see if we could help Indian recover. I found the president away on a vacation or holiday on a boat, or yacht at the beach for two weeks or so. I've always felt that when things get tough, it is the time to roll up sleeves and go to work. Yet while the ship was sinking, the skipper was away! Wasn't it Nero who fiddled while Rome burned?"

Clymer went on to propose that it was not too late to resurrect a traditional but improved V-twin Scout and manufacture it in Springfield. Recent Indian news releases had given no hope that the furnaces would be relighted at the Springfield factory. Rather, they touted J. Brockhouse & Company's previous record of international success as a motorcycle marketing firm. In response to these claims, Clymer continued:

> "Brockhouse may be justly proud of their record of industrial leadership in 37 other countries, but we are not proud of their record in America—in fact, a lot of Americans are mad—darned mad—at what

### VICTORY AT DAYTONA

*Already committed to its new lightweight line of motorcycles, Indian produced the 648 Scout in 1948 as a stopgap measure against the advancing wave of Harley-Davidson motorcycles on the nation's racetracks. The 648, known as the "Big Base Scout" for its enlarged oil sump, and subsequently as the "Daytona Scout," was only produced in limited quantity. However, the project paid off when Floyd Emde won the prestigious Daytona 200. On Emde's left is his wife, Florence. Pictured on Emde's right in the Daytona winner's circle is Ralph Rogers, who attempted to take the company in a new direction. Indian's racing program under Rogers was shifted to overhead-valve Warrior TT prototypes in 1949, ending in a total disaster at Laconia where 12 machines were entered and 12 failed to finish. Although AMA Class C racing rules stipulated that racing machines be based on serial-production motorcycles, no more than 50 Big Base Scouts were ever manufactured. Some experts maintain that a total of only 50 engines were built, and that no more than 25 complete machines were assembled.*

## 1949 ARROW

When a group headed by Ralph B. Rogers bought Indian in 1945, a plan was devised to totally reinvent the company in an effort to better position it against the British lightweights that had begun to flood the American market. Indian purchased Torque Manufacturing, where a new engine had been in development since the early 1940s. Torque's concept was to build engines for a whole line of motorcycles by using multiples of a single 220-cc overhead-valve upper end. Major components such as connecting rods, pistons, cylinders, heads, and valvetrains would be used on all models. With this "modular" concept it would be able to produce a 220-cc single, a 440-cc twin, and an 880-cc four-cylinder. The Indian Arrow, introduced in 1949, was the first stage of the product line, a 220-cc single. The motorcycle incorporated the latest chassis and suspension designs and featured liberal use of light alloys, including a chrome moly frame. It weighed only 240 pounds. Rogers hoped to create a whole new "gentleman motorcyclist" market, not unlike what Honda achieved later when it aimed its products at "the nicest people." Rogers envisioned young, upscale fathers buying 440-cc Indian Scouts, and giving their sons 220-cc Arrows. The V-twin Chief would continue to be Indian's product for the traditional American motorcyclist. Although the concept was fundamentally sound—as proven by the Japanese over a decade later—Indian's effort to rush the all-new product into the market resulted in manufacturing problems and poor quality control. The new Indians were very unreliable and earned a terrible reputation even before the factory could move into serious production. The 1949 Indian Arrow pictured is owned by Bob Schingler.

*'successful' Brockhouse has done to Indian. Our heavy mail indicates that other motorcycle enthusiasts in this country feel exactly the same way about Indian as we do."*

Clymer sent a copy of his editorial to John Brockhouse in England. Brockhouse fired back a letter, accusing Clymer of only making matters worse for Indian, and aggrandizing his own investment in the company. Clymer responded, and this time his references to the "successful Brockhouse" fairly dripped with sarcasm. Both letters were published in the June 1954 issue of *Cycle Magazine.* But it was to no avail. There was nothing that Floyd Clymer or any other Indian enthusiast could do to persuade John Brockhouse to resume the manufacture of a real American Indian. That same year, Hollywood produced the notorious film *The Wild One,* starring Marlon Brando, which inscribed in the American imagination a dark and negative image of motorcycling that would plague the industry for the next 40 years. So much for Ralph Rogers' concept of the gentleman motorcyclist.

Brockhouse continued to exploit Indian's powerful brand name. Money was allocated to racing teams on Norton and Matchless motorcycles with riders who carried "Indian" on their racing jerseys. From 1955 through 1959, the Indian nameplate was affixed to Royal Enfields with model names like Tomahawk, Trailblazer, Woodsman, and Fire Arrow. The Brockhouse team even tried to sell a Chief, which was a 700-cc Royal Enfield with fat tires intended to make it pass as a touring motorcycle. These efforts were insufficient even against their British-made competitors, since Triumph and BSA had become the dominant and reputable brands. Failing to benefit from the Indian connection, in 1961 Enfield announced that the brand would henceforth appear "stripped of its feathers and war paint."

In 1959 the remaining assets of the company passed on to Associated Motorcycles, Ltd., builders of Matchless and AJS motorcycles. In a token effort to keep the Indian image alive, Matchless sold a model named Apache in the American market only. The dealer network became "Matchless-Indian" dealers, but they sold only Matchless motorcycles.

It is likely that the only thing John Brockhouse ever wanted from Indian was its dealer network in America, and having gained that, there was no further reason to try to keep the marque alive. Indian traditionalists deride Ralph Rogers as the man who destroyed Indian by building an un-American and untraditional motorcycle. However, if one looks honestly at the state to which the company had been allowed to decline by 1945, it is not likely that Rogers could have succeeded through any other strategy. When he acquired control of the company, it was manufacturing one outdated model and was saddled with the overhead of an antiquated factory that had been running at 5 percent capacity for decades. The modular engine concept was not an unsound concept from a manufacturing and marketing point of view. Given the opportunity to succeed, it could have brought forth a modern Indian Four 15 years ahead of Honda's revolutionary four-cylinder motorcycle.

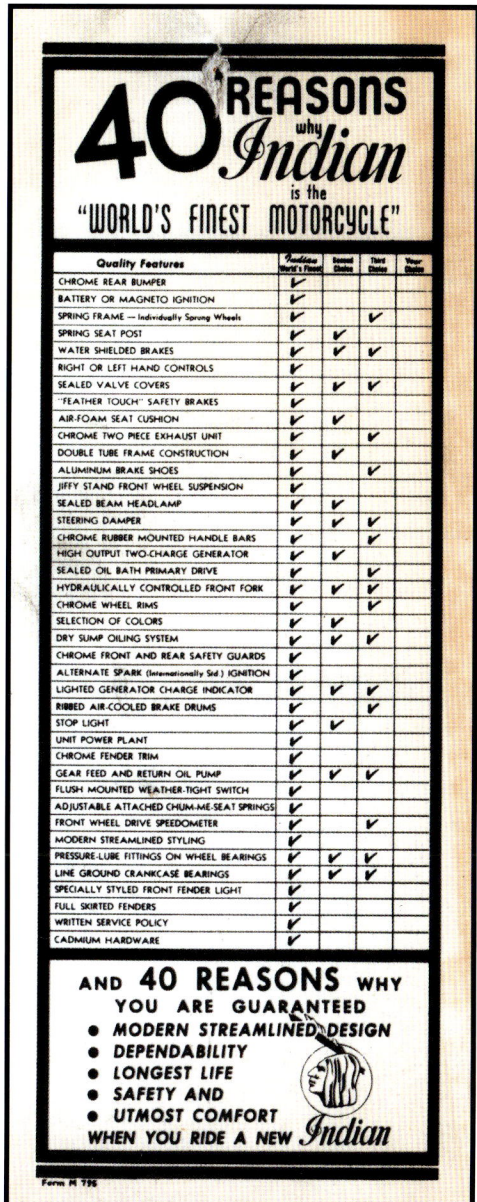

In retrospect, we can recognize that the vision for which Ralph Rogers has been criticized was really not so different from the vision for which Soichiro Honda has been hailed as one of the great geniuses of our age. Rogers' desire to identify and sell to the gentleman motorcyclists of America is not so different from Honda's belief that "You meet the nicest people on a Honda." In Honda's case it became a self-fulfilling prophecy, and motorcycling was forever changed along the lines that Rogers himself had envisioned. But there were two differences. Honda's product was brought to a high level of performance and quality before it was introduced to the American market. And Honda benefited from the very economic forces that militated against Rogers and Indian.

Indian, under the leadership of Ralph Rogers, can be criticized for rushing a new product into production without adequate testing. It can be criticized for trying to relocate a factory at the same time it was trying to manufacture a new product. But had it done everything right, it is unlikely that Indian could have ever overcome the devaluation of the British pound within months after introducing a motorcycle designed to compete with British products. As had happened so many times in the past—with Henry Ford's introduction of the moving assembly line, installment credit, and higher wages in 1913 and 1914; with the erection of tariffs in Europe in 1920; with the stock market crash in 1929; with the invention of the military Jeep in 1943—the American motorcycle industry found itself battered by competitive, economic, and political forces beyond its control. Such was the case with Indian, the marque that earned and still holds a grand place in the memory and imagination of motorcycle enthusiasts throughout the world.

## The Indians That Might Have Been

Over its half-century as a motorcycle manufacturer, Indian built most of its American motorcycles around only three engine designs: the De Dion–based engine, designed by Oscar Hedstrom; the Powerplus, designed by the Gustafsons; and the Scout, designed by Charles Franklin. While Indian introduced several small-bore engines, these motorcycles did not sell well and were produced only in small quantities. The Four and Torque engines were acquired technology, developed outside the Wigwam. Thus, from 1901 until the last Chief in 1953, the vast majority of Indians sold relied on side-valve technology.

Perhaps the technological watershed for Indian in its rivalry with Harley-Davidson was 1936, with the introduction of Harley's overhead-valve Model EL—the Knucklehead. At a time when both companies were weathering economic recession and a weak motorcycle market, Harley-Davidson took the risk of investing in updating the valvetrain of its traditional engine technology. Indian, on the other hand, hunkered down and focused on reducing its research and development and manufacturing costs. How could it have been different had Indian pursued a more aggressive development strategy?

We can fantasize that had Indian chosen to build a "Knuckle-beater," it might have been something like the Crocker, manufactured in Los Angeles between 1936 and 1941. Albert Crocker, born in 1882, joined the Indian engineering department in 1909

following a stint with Aurora Automatic Machine. After holding a number of posts with Indian, he resigned to become an Indian dealer in 1924, first in Kansas City, then later in Los Angeles. He also owned a machine shop, which was an Indian supplier. With shop foreman Paul Bigsby as a partner, he developed and manufactured a high-performance engine for speedway racing.

In 1935, Crocker and Bigsby began to develop a high-performance street and touring machine, based on what Bigsby had learned from fitting 101 Scouts with special cylinders and overhead-valve cylinder heads of his own design. They produced a prototype of the Crocker motorcycle in 1936, the same year that the Knucklehead arrived on the scene. It was an overhead-valve V-twin with hemispherical combustion chambers. The lower end was very similar to an Indian. It was a robust, noisy, exciting, somewhat uncivilized, and hard-starting machine capable of cruising at 90 miles per

### INDIAN TRIES STAR POWER

*Indian tried to use star power to launch its revolutionary "Dyna-Torque" Lightweights. Tying Indian's new image to American heroes was part of Indian President Ralph Rogers' strategy to appeal to a new market of "gentleman motorcyclists." It might have worked, as it did for Soichiro Honda a decade later, except production problems destroyed the reputation of Indian's new design, and international economics put the brand at a competitive price disadvantage against the British lightweights that had begun to flood the American market.*

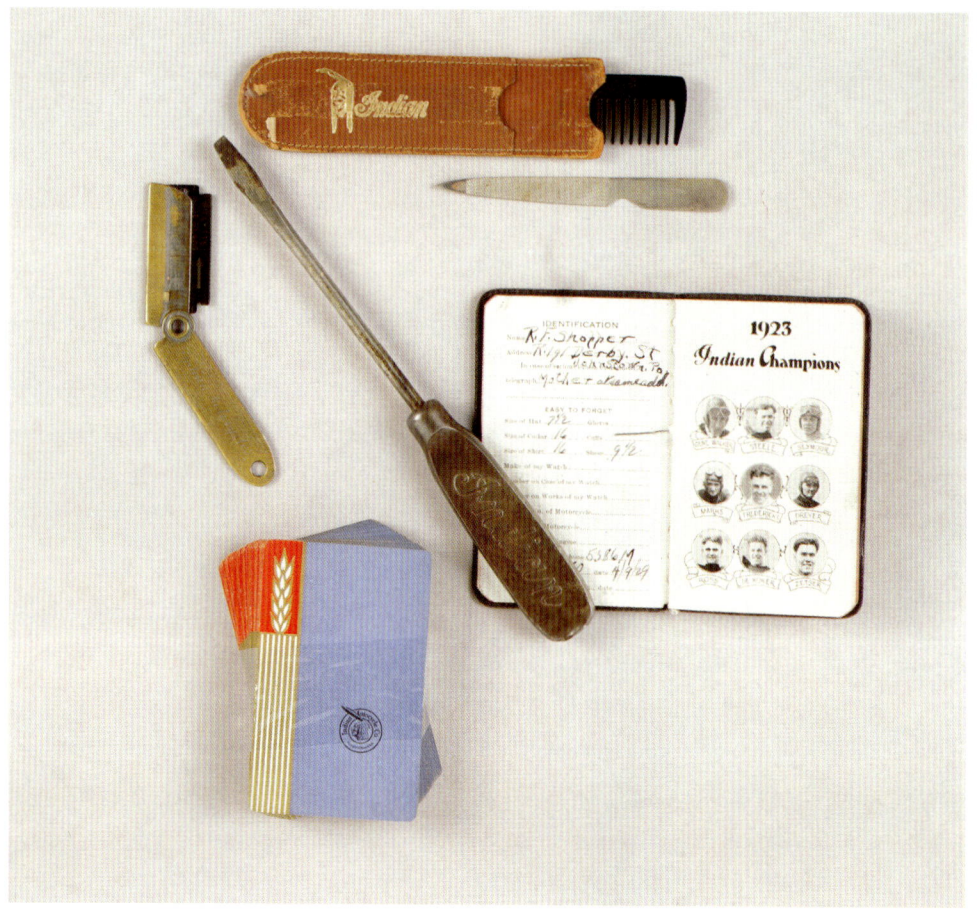

**INDIAN EPHEMERA**
*Clockwise from top center: An Indian comb and nail file grooming kit in a leather case, a pocket notebook featuring Indian's 1923 champions, a screwdriver, a deck of cards, and a razor blade holder.*

hour with a top speed above 100. It was to touring motorcycles of the day what a Dodge Viper is to modern touring automobiles, easily capable of stirring the blood of any young enthusiast who wished to run rings around a Harley.

The Crocker was expensive compared to top-of-the line Indians and Harleys, and it is estimated that only about 100 were ever built. Throughout his venture as an American motorcycle manufacturer, Albert Crocker remained friendly with his Indian colleagues, and in 1940 offered to sell his design and manufacturing rights to Indian. Had Indian acquired the Crocker engine, it might have found a way to civilize it somewhat and bring it to market in a sporting machine capable of outperforming any Harley-Davidson of the era.

At the expense of the War Department, Indian had an opportunity in the 1940s to develop a shaft-driven motorcycle, which appeared as the military Model 841. Although it still employed old side-valve technology, the longitudinally mounted V-twin gave Indian the makings of a shaft drive touring machine that could have rivaled the BMW motorcycles that came to prominence in the postwar civilian market. And such a bike would have outclassed anything in the Harley-Davidson line for design sophistication.

This possibility was illustrated by more than one Indian enthusiast who took the 841, polished its engine cases, installed Chief skirted fenders, and added some brightwork, resulting in a very attractive, modern touring motorcycle. But Indian did nothing with the equity it had in the Model 841. To the contrary, it chose to neglect its big bike touring market entirely in favor of its new lightweight vertical singles and twins. However, it is clear that at one point Indian realized it had an engineering asset in the 841. In 1944 it produced the prototype X44, a shaft-driven, inline four that utilized the 841 frame and powertrain. It was a compact and sleek motorcycle with two cylinders exhausting on each side, but the project was abandoned when Ralph Rogers took Indian in a different direction.

After Indian linked up with J. Brockhouse, Ltd., a new-concept Chief containing a Vincent engine was exhibited. This was, in fact, a simple, brilliant, and logical idea. Indian needed new engine technology to compete with Harley-Davidson in the touring market, and the Vincent

provided the most advanced, powerful, and respected V-twin engine available. The 1,000-cc Vincent engine came in various states of tune, but the slowest model in the line—the Rapide—was capable of achieving 110 miles per hour. The Black Shadow could achieve 125 miles per hour, and in 1952, a modified Black Lightning set an American land speed record of 156.58 miles per hour.

Indian sent a Chief frame to England where a Series B Rapide engine was installed. It was a relatively simple fit, and the running prototype exceeded 100 miles per hour. Not only would the Vincent have had the power and speed to make Indian king of the postwar interstate highways, but it even looked right. Its bulk and large, deeply finned cylinders fit nicely with Indian's overall styling. But a "Vindian" Chief never appeared, in part because Vincent—like Indian—was in its final days.

Given these hypothetical examples, it is interesting to speculate what Indian might have produced, had it not abandoned its V-twin and four-cylinder traditions, and

**THE ENFIELD INDIANS**

*Production was not resumed at the Wigwam in 1954, so John Brockhouse began to supply his American dealer network with British Royal Enfields dressed up as Indians. This brochure from 1955 introduces Enfield's 250-cc and 500-cc singles and 700-cc twins under the Indian brand. Later a 700-cc model was outfitted with fat tires and floorboards and called an Indian Chief. The Enfield Indians were not well accepted in the American market. They offended Indian traditionalists, and their performance and quality were below competitive British brands.*

**THE TORQUE FOUR**

*Had Indian's idea of a new, lightweight gentleman's motorcycle not gone awry, the company might have soon introduced a modern overhead-valve four-cylinder, because such a motorcycle was in prototype development. The Torque Four featured a longitudinally mounted engine with shaft drive. The cylinders and heads were turned 90 degrees from their positioning on the Arrow and Scout models. Camshafts ran down both sides of the engine to facilitate this layout. Pictured is the actual Torque Four prototype, owned by Dr. John Patt.*

had it explored options more logical and less radical than its do-or-die commitment to the Dyna-Torque small-bore modular engines that appeared in 1948.

## Indian's Brave Warriors

Even before automobiles drove motorcycles out of the American transportation market in the 1920s, motorcycles appealed to people interested in speed, performance, technology, and excitement. Throughout American motorcycle history, the most successful brands have invested heavily in racing and endurance competitions to

garner publicity, gain prestige, and get bragging rights about technological superiority. It was certainly no exception with Indian, which established a reputation in both national and world-class competition within its first decade. Even when it was clear that Harley-Davidson had won the war in the commercial market, with better technology and far more money to invest in racing, Indian die-hards aboard their trusty Sport Scouts kept winning major races and national titled events. Below are some of the men and women whose exploits in the competitive arena helped establish Indian as one of the greatest motorcycle brands of all time.

**INDIAN EPHEMERA**

*Indian smoking accessories: match books, a lighter, metal match box safes, and a cigar cutter.*

Within months after the first serial production motorcycles began to come out of the factory in 1902, Indian won the first endurance competition ever held in America, a race from Boston to New York. As a former champion bicycle racer, **George Hendee** had competition in his blood. In another major endurance event, run from New York to Springfield and back in July 1904, he earned a gold medal, along with fellow riders **Oscar Hedstrom** and **George Holden.** In 1903, **George Holden** rode an Indian to victory in the nation's first long-distance track race, covering more than 150 miles in four hours.

The famous and popular racer **Jake DeRosier** earned his first victory for Indian in 1905 at a half-mile track in Cambridge, Massachusetts, setting a new 46-mile-per-hour speed record. That same year, DeRosier completed the steep Mount Washington 8-mile hillclimb in just under 21 minutes, beating every automobile entered except a 60-horsepower racer that bested him by less than a second. DeRosier's exploits also included setting a 100-mile speed record at Playa Del Rey, California, losing the title and then regaining it from fellow Indian rider **Morty Graves.** Although DeRosier did not figure in the one-two-three sweep of Indians at the Isle of Man in 1911, just a week later he set an 87-mile-per-hour record and beat British ace Charles Collier in two out of three match races at Brooklands.

In July 1906, **Stanley Kellog** rode an Indian to victory at an annual endurance run sanctioned by the FAM, and Indian dealers **Louis Mueller** and **George Holden** set a transcontinental record of 31.5 days. Indian's first great international endurance victory came in 1907 when **T. K. "Teddy" Hastings** won a prestigious 1,000-mile trial in England. This event was the predecessor of the International Six Days Trial, where in 1908 Indian-mounted Hastings became the first American to win a gold medal.

In 1908, **B. A. Swenson** set a Chicago-to-New York record of 33 hours, 26 minutes. He traversed the 978 miles on Indian's new 3.5 horsepower Hedstrom engine with the mechanically actuated intake valve.

On August 14, 1909, **Erwin "Cannonball" Baker** won the FAM Ten Mile Amateur Championship at the first race ever held at the Indianapolis Motor Speedway. On August 14, 1911 he shook the hand of President William Howard Taft after winning the Presidents Cup at another Indianapolis-area race track.

**Earl Armstrong,** who later became Indian production manager, won a 300-mile board track championship for Indian in 1909.

In addition to its victorious 1911 Isle of Man sweep, delivered by **Oliver Godfrey, Charles B. Franklin**, and **A. J. Moorehouse**, Indian earned prestigious titles in national competition as well. Departing San Francisco on June 26, 1911, **Volney Davis** reduced America's transcontinental record to 20 days, 9 hours, and 11 minutes. And in 1912, Irishman **Charles Franklin** set four separate speed records at Brooklands, traveling 300 miles in less than 300 minutes.

Cannonball Baker, who was much larger than most motorcycle track racers of the day, switched to endurance riding in 1914, completing his first transcontinental attempt aboard an Indian in 11 days, 12 hours, and 10 minutes. Other long-distance records by Baker were the Canada-to-Mexico Three Flags Run, which he completed in 1915 in 3.5 days on a Powerplus prototype; and a second transcontinental record in 1922 aboard an Ace Four, the predecessor to the Indian Four. Baker also held world endurance records for 12 and 24 hours, and speed records for 500- and 1,000-mile distances. Baker was given his nickname by a New York journalist who compared him to the Cannonball Express train. In 1916, Baker embarked on a South Pacific tour that resulted in 13 new long-distance records in Hawaii, Australia, and Tasmania, including a 1,000 miles-in-24-hours feat of endurance.

The first of the great Dodge City 300-mile races took place in 1914, and it was won by Indian rider **Glen "Slivers" Boyd**. The following season **Ray Crevison** became dominant on the flat tracks on behalf of Indian, beating the mighty Cyclone of **Don Johns** who would come over to ride for the Wigwam in 1916.

**Gene Walker** won his first race aboard an Indian in 1912, then took his first national championship at Saratoga, New York, in 1915. Following World War I, Walker became practically unbeatable, winning 6 out of 13 national championships for Indian in 1919, setting three track records in the process. He also set a world speed record of 103.56 miles per hour aboard an eight-valve Indian at Daytona Beach in 1920. Walker won two more nationals for Indian in the new 30.50-inch racing class (500-cc) in 1924.

In 1916, **Adeline and Augusta Van Buren** became the first women to ride solo machines from coast to coast (the mother-daughter team of Avis and Effie Hotchkiss had ridden a Harley-Davidson sidecar rig from New York to San Francisco in 1915). The Van Buren sisters also rode their new Powerplus Indians to the top of Pikes Peak during their transcontinental trip.

Also in 1916, **Myron Warner** won the inaugural running of the famous Capistrano Hillclimb aboard a Powerplus.

**INDIAN EPHEMERA**
*Indian mechanical pencils, a leather coin purse, and a ring.*

**INDIAN EPHEMERA**

*Indian tie bars, fobs, and lapel pins.*

In 1920 at Beverly Hills, California, **Albert "Shrimp" Burns**—riding a stock Powerplus—became the first man to win a championship at over 100 miles per hour. Later that year he rode his side-valve Indian to victory over the eight-valve Harley-Davidson of Jim Davis. During the 1920 season, Indian won 14 national championship races.

**Herbert LeVack** set kilometer and mile records at over 95 miles per hour at Brooklands in 1920. In 1921 he rode his Powerplus to victory at the 500-mile race at Brooklands, the longest race in England.

Switching from Harley-Davidson to Indian in 1922, **Jim Davis** recorded the fastest lap to date on a board track, clocking 110.67 miles per hour! Davis won six national championships for Indian in 1928 and 1929.

In May 1923 **Paul Remaly** set out with his 600-cc Scout to break the Three Flags record, then held by Henderson. Remaly completed the ride in 46 hours and 58 minutes. Wells Bennet came back in June for Henderson, lowering the record to 46 hours and 9 minutes. Remaly promptly responded in July by reducing the record to 43 hours and 21 minutes. Then in August, Remaly set a new transcontinental record of 5 days, 17 hours, and 10 minutes, beating the previous Henderson record by nearly a full day.

In 1926, **Johnny Seymoure** set a 30.50-ci record of 112.63 miles per hour and a 61-ci record of 132 miles per hour at Daytona Beach. With the United States no longer a member of the international federation, these records did not become official. Seymoure's speed for the 61-ci class was 23 miles per hour faster than the current recognized world record! That same year, **Curly Fredricks** set the all-time fastest board track record at 120.3 miles per hour. Fredricks was riding an Indian with a 61-ci side-valve engine. Indian won 8 of 12 national championships in 1926. That same year, 16-year-old **Bob Armstrong,** son of track-racing champion Earl Armstrong, rode an Altoona-engine Indian to the AMA national amateur hillclimbing championship.

During the Depression, hillclimbing became even more popular than track racing. Both Indian and Harley-Davidson supported factory hillclimbing teams. Some of Indian's great hillclimbers were **Gene Rhyne, Orie Steele,** and **Howard Mitzel.** In 1931, Rhyne won every national event in the 45-ci class. Over a 40-year career, Mitzel won championships in 1936, 1939, 1949, 1952, and 1953.

In 1934 the AMA's modern era of Class C racing began. It was a class in which the Indian Sport Scout engine excelled. The greatest racer of the era was **Ed "Iron Man" Kretz,** who came into national prominence when he won the Savannah 200-miler in 1936. In 1937 the 200-mile road race moved to its new home, Daytona Beach, where Ed Kretz won the first Daytona. Although Kretz never carried the AMA Number 1 Plate (which in this era was awarded to the winner of the annual Springfield

Mile), he won on almost every track on the national circuit. He won Langhorne four times and was elected the AMA's most popular rider in 1938 and 1948.

In 1936, **Lester Hillbish** won Langhorne for Indian. Six of the top 10 Langhorne finishers were aboard Indian Scouts. The following year, Hillbish won four championships, setting two track records and earning the AMA Number 1 Plate by virtue of his victory at Springfield, Illinois.

Also in 1936, **Rody Rodenburg** lowered the transcontinental record to 71 hours and 20 minutes aboard a Sport Scout, and **L. C. Smith** set a transcontinental sidecar record of 86 hours, 55 minutes.

In 1938, Indian won eight of the 12 AMA national championship races. Kretz and the **Castonguay brothers, Woodsie** and **Frenchie** dominated. Kretz won Langhorne and the inaugural Laconia. Woodsie Castonguay set records at Reading and Springfield, capturing the coveted AMA Number 1 Plate for the second consecutive year. Frenchie Castonguay set a track record at Topsfield, Massachusetts. **Rollie Free** set two speed records at Daytona Beach: 109.65 miles per hour with a 74-ci Chief, and 111.55 miles per hour with a 45-ci Scout. **Fred Ludlow** upped Free's 45-ci record to 115.126 later that year at Bonneville, and upped the 74-ci record to 120.747 miles per hour.

In 1939, **Stan Wittinski** won Springfield to give Indian its third consecutive AMA Number 1 Plate. **Melvin Rhoades** followed in 1940 to make it four times in a row. **Ted Edwards** won two championship events in 1940 aboard an Indian Chief.

When racing resumed after World War II, Ed Kretz put Indian back in the winner's circle at Laconia, and **Johnny Spiegelhoff** won Langhorne. One of Indian's great postwar personalities was **Max Bubeck.** Bubeck had come on the scene just before the war at land speed record events and with a Novice class win at the Greenhorn Enduro in 1937. However, Bubeck came into his prominence in 1947 when he won the Greenhorn Enduro outright aboard an Indian Four. In 1948 he set a 135.58-mile-per-hour speed record at Rosamond Dry Lake aboard his notorious "Chout" (a hopped-up Chief engine in a 101 Scout chassis). A die-hard Indian fan, Bubeck even achieved speed-tuning success with the 1949 vertical twin Scouts, and some of his learning went into the 500-cc Warrior TT when it appeared in 1950. In 1962, Bubeck won the Greenhorn again, this time aboard a 1950 Warrior!

**INDIAN EPHEMERA**

*Indian lapel pins and dealer convention mementos.*

**CHARLES FRANKLIN**

*Irishman Charles B. Franklin finished second in Indian's 1911 one-two-three sweep of the Isle of Man. Later he earned speed records at Brooklands and learned speed tuning secrets. Retiring from racing in 1914, he went to work at Indian's Dublin distributorship in 1915, then joined Indian's engineering department in Springfield in 1916. Franklin was the designer of the Scout engine and the legendary 101 Scout motorcycle. His wizardry at speed tuning side-valve engines practically made obsolete the eight-valve factory racers. Franklin left Indian due to poor health in 1930, and died in 1932 at the age of 46.*
*Photo courtesy of Jerry Hatfield.*

In 1948, Indian introduced the 648 Scout, known as the Big Base Scout. **Floyd Emde** won the first postwar Daytona aboard a Big Base Scout at a record speed of 84.1 miles per hour. **Joe Gee** won the Jack Pine Enduro in 1951 aboard a Warrior TT.

Indian's final racing glory was earned by a threesome known as the Indian Wrecking Crew: **Bobby Hill, Bill Tuman,** and **Ernie Beckman.** Using the V-twin Scouts, this team achieved dirt-track championship victories for Indian after its technology had been displaced by the Harley-Davidson WR. Hill won Milwaukee in 1951 and Springfield in both 1951 and 1952, returning the AMA Number 1 Plate to Indian two more times. Tuman won Bay Meadows in 1952, and Hill won Syracuse. In 1953, Hill won three championships, and Tuman won Springfield, giving Indian its last AMA Number 1 Plate. On October 11, 1953, Beckman won at Williams Grove, Pennsylvania, giving Indian its last AMA victory.

One of Indian's most colorful competitors was New Zealander **Bert Munro.** Munro campaigned a streamliner at Bonneville from 1962 through 1967, powered by a highly modified engine that had begun life as a 1923 Scout! With this machine, he achieved a speed of 190.070 miles per hour, the fastest speed ever traveled by an Indian.

## The Battle of the Brand

Writing about the history of Indian in *Motorcyclist* in 1951, John J. O'Connor asserted, "Looking back over the half-century since Indian was born, no more popular or wealth-producing name could have been chosen." He could not possibly have known how that statement would ring true, even into the present day. Although an Indian motorcycle was not manufactured in America from 1954 to 1999, the marque remains so strong that men have lost fortunes, destroyed their businesses, wrecked friendships, and gone to federal prison in pursuit of the trademark, or through their desire to control and exploit it.

In 1962, Associated Motors sold its American operations to Berliner Motors Corporation, which made no further attempt to exploit the Indian brand name. Then in 1968, Floyd Clymer, who had by this time sold *Cycle Magazine*, launched a motorcycle-importing venture and began to affix the familiar Indian script name to motorcycles with Enfield and Velocette engines bolted into Italian-made frames. Although Clymer had made no effort to secure legal ownership of the marque, his use of it was not contested. The venture was not successful, and very few Clymer Indians were sold. Upon Clymer's death, his widow sold the presumed trademark rights to the Indian Motorcycle Company of Gardena, California, which affixed the name to Taiwan-built minibikes. This company failed in 1976, and from 1978 through 1990, American Moped Associates attempted to sell Spanish and Taiwan-built products as Indians.

Next appeared Philip S. Zanghi, who announced in 1992 that he would soon produce 100,000 motorcycles per year at a factory in Connecticut, claiming his new Indian would have a titanium engine and antilock brakes. Zanghi claimed to own the Indian trademark and declared his mission was to return pride and jobs to America.

At the time of Zanghi's statement, Harley-Davidson was producing fewer than 70,000 motorcycles per year. How Zanghi was going to bring a new Indian into such huge annual production in just a few months without ever having built a prototype was never explained. Not surprisingly, Zanghi did not build any Indian motorcycles, but he did make licensing deals affixing Indian's proud logo to banjos and cigars. Zanghi's pronouncements triggered a flurry of legal claims and counterclaims over who owned the Indian logo. Eventually Zanghi was indicted and imprisoned for fraud in 1997.

In 1994, Wayne Baughman's Indian Motorcycle Manufacturing Inc (IMMI). produced two 100-ci (1,640-cc) V-twin prototypes. These bikes were not even near a preproduction prototype stage. Their engines appeared to be machined entirely from billet, and they were never seen running for more than a few minutes. While Baughman took the position that "Indian" had passed into public domain, he avoided a trademark dispute by calling his product the Century Chief. It had Indian-style skirted fenders and an Indian head on the front fender. Baughman reportedly raised $5 million for his project, and at one point his facility was fire-bombed. Some speculated that the bombing had been by upset Century Chief customers who had placed deposits but not received motorcycles. Others speculated that Baughman himself had caused the explosion for an excuse not to deliver his yet-to-be-built motorcycles to customers. Whatever the case, Baughman disappeared, and his Century Chief never went into production. IMMI went into receivership.

In 1997, Eller Industries, owned by Lonnie Labriola, who had been an investor in IMMI, partnered with the Cow Creek Band of the Umpqua Indian Tribe to manufacture a new American Indian motorcycle on tribal land. Experienced motor industry personalities brought aboard as consultants included Robert Lutz, former vice chairman of Chrysler, and James Parker of Roush Industries. A mock-up, featuring its own proprietary V-twin engine, was created. Eller, however, was challenged for the trademark by the Toronto-based Indian Motorcycle Company. In November 1998, Indian Motorcycle Company purchased the California Motorcycle Company, builder of CMC motorcycles, powered by S&S engines, commonly referred to as Harley-Davidson Evolution engine "clones." The new company, named the Indian Motorcycle Company of Gilroy, California, prevailed in court and won the right to control the disputed and valuable Indian name and trademarks, largely because it had a running prototype and was ready to go into production with a new Indian motorcycle. This company is still being challenged in court by the Cow Creek Band, which seeks royalties under the Indian Arts and Crafts Act, prohibiting non-indigenous parties from exploiting the American Indian culture.

The Indian Motorcycle Company has worked with the rolling chassis already developed and manufactured by the California Motorcycle Company, and has applied sheet

**PAUL DU PONT**

*Eleuthere Paul du Pont was born in 1887. At the age of 16, he constructed his own motorcycle, mounting a de Dion-type engine on a bicycle chassis. He became a mechanical engineer and owned marine engine and motorcar businesses before assuming control of Indian in 1930. Du Pont divested Indian of its unprofitable sidelines, such as the manufacture of outboard motors, and focused on returning the company to profitability. Du Pont guided Indian through the difficult decade of the Great Depression, and sold the company in 1945. Du Pont died in 1950. Here he is pictured showing his home-made motor bicycle to motorcycle journalist Chet Billings.*

**1950–1951 WARRIOR:**

*In an attempt to enter the fray of AMA championship racing, in 1950 Indian produced a 500-cc model called the Warrior, and a higher-performance version called the Warrior TT. The introduction of this model was also a disaster. Twelve Warrior TT prototypes were entered at the Laconia road race in 1949, and all 12 failed to finish. Although the Warrior TT that came into production got high praise in the motorcycle press, it was too little and too late. The reputation of the new product was damaged beyond repair, and the company had no money for further development, advertising, or public relations damage control. In January 1950, the company came under the control of British investor and motorcycle importer John Brockhouse, who showed more interest in importing British motorcycles than in manufacturing Indians. The Warrior depicted here is a 1951 model owned by Pete Bollenbach. It has appeared previously in the Motorcycle Hall of Fame Museum.*

metal and other design features to create a new Indian motorcycle complete with deep-skirted fenders. Its first model was the 1999 Limited Edition Chief. In 2000 it introduced the Millennium Chief, and in 2001 it added a Scout and a model called the Spirit to its line. The 2001 product line also includes a Sport Scout which, surprisingly, has a rigid frame. Reminiscent of the low-slung 101 Scout, it is a daring departure in the modern riding environment, in which comfort is expected of luxury cruisers.

Traditional Indian fans have criticized these new products because they are powered by S&S engines that look exactly like Harley-Davidson engines. Indian partisans have never been enthusiastic about the many latter-day attempts to resurrect the brand, but they can be especially uncharitable toward a motorcycle that looks like classic Indian styling around a Harley engine. However, in the new company's defense, the Denver court awarding the rights to the Indian trademark placed a time limitation on bringing a product to market, and IMC argues that it had to use a readily available engine. It says it chose the S&S, manufactured in Viola, Wisconsin, for its high quality. IMC claims to have a proprietary engine in development, and currently in testing, though no details are available at this time.

The motorcycles have excellent fit and finish and are reported to be high-performance machines. Like the Indians of the 1930s and 1940s, they are bright and handsome, with the Chief available in 12 color combinations. The Scout especially has been praised by the motorcycle press for its speed and good handling.

Retailing through a network of approximately 230 dealers, the new Indian Motorcycle Company produced over 6,000 units during its first two years, and is expecting to produce 6,200 units during 2001. If IMC is successful in introducing its own engine, there will be no justification to further challenge its claim to be the first true American-manufactured Indian to appear since the Wigwam in Springfield, Massachusetts, ceased production 48 years ago.

## The Indelible Indian

With the arrival of Indian's 100th anniversary, clubs and enthusiasts throughout the world have begun mounting celebrations of the Century of Indian. In addition to the two-year featured exhibit at the Motorcycle Hall of Fame Museum in Pickerington, Ohio, clubs all over America, Europe, and the South Pacific have honored the legendary Indian motorcycle. Everything will be on parade—1902 Hedstrom-powered singles, Powerplus models of the teens, beautiful Sport Scouts of the 1930s, the mighty Chiefs and Fours of the 1940s, the Dyna-Torque singles and twins from the American Indian's final days, the Brockhouse and Clymer branded Indians, and the current California-built

**RETAILING IN THE 1920s**

*A typical motorcycle dealership, circa 1920, featuring Indian, Henderson, and Excelsior motorcycles. The Powerplus on the left would indicate the photo was taken after 1916. In the doorway is a motorwheel equipped bicycle.*

**BRIGGS WEAVER AND RALPH ROGERS**
*Briggs Weaver, right, was brought in as Indian's design chief by Paul du Pont. He left Indian to join Torque Manufacturing in 1943 after giving Indian its famous streamlined styling. Ralph Rogers, right, headed the investment group that purchased Indian from du Pont in 1945. Shortly thereafter, Indian acquired Torque Manufacturing and Weaver returned to the Wigwam to head up its revolutionary Dyna-Torque project. Weaver left Indian in 1948; Rogers in 1950. Photo courtesy of Jerry Hatfield.*

renditions. They will all be brought out, shined up, and ridden in celebration of what their owners indisputably believe is the greatest motorcycle marque of all time.

What is it that engenders loyalty, anger, longing, romance, nostalgia, and desperate attempts to resurrect the Indian motorcycle after nearly a half-century? What is so powerful about this motorcycle that a thriving cottage industry has survived to provide parts for pre-1945 Indians? Why do Americans who know practically nothing about motorcycling know about Indian and buy into the belief that it was one of the greatest motorcycles ever made? Why has the Indian motorcycle become indelible in our American collective consciousness? Perhaps it is for no other reason than the unforgettable impression left by the imposing style of the classic Indians that appeared in 1940 and thereafter.

Prior to 1930, America was largely a nonplayer in the world of style and design, dominated previously by the German Bauhaus and Paris-based Art Deco schools. But between the world wars, America suddenly emerged as a new and leading influence, largely as a result of its industrial might. The United States made two great contributions to international style and design. These were the skyscraper and streamlining. In a sense, they were almost opposites—one emphasizing vertical lines and the other emphasizing horizontal lines—but they both expressed the nation's expansive and urgent mood to grow and express itself, and both are typified by sleekness.

America's sleek new schools of design were epitomized in architecture by the Chrysler Building, designed by William Van Alan; in automobiles by the Auburn 851 Speedster, the Cord 810, and the Duesenberg Beverly, designed by Gordon Buehrig; in rail travel by the streamlined New York Central Hudson-class and Penn Central locomotives, designed by Raymond Loewy; and in motorcycles by the streamlined and skirted Indians designed by Briggs Weaver.

The essence of streamlining is to make moving objects go faster by reducing wind resistance. The essence of the streamlined style is to make objects look quick and

moving, even when they are sitting still. This was achieved in the 1940 Indian, perhaps as well as or even better than Buehrig's cars or Loewy's locomotives. Furthermore, the streamlined Indian had no stylistic competitors. Prior to the arrival of current-day copycats, no one else in the motorcycle industry ever came close to imitating or matching the audacious image of the classic American Indian.

Many enthusiast organizations deserve credit for helping keep the Indian marque alive. These include the Antique Motorcycle Club of America; the Indian 101 Scout Association; the Indian Four Cylinder Motorcycle Club; the Springfield Indian Motorcycle Club; the All-American Indian Motorcycle Club; the Indian Motorcycle Club International; and others throughout the world, including the Indian Owners Group of New Zealand; the Indian Club of the Netherlands; and groups in England, Canada, France, Scotland, and Germany.

Is there any wonder we can't forget the fabulous American Indian? Is there any likelihood we ever will?

**READY TO RACE**

*Six Indians in a row. What appear to be stock Hedstrom twins line up for racing at the Dunbar, West Virginia fairgrounds, circa 1912. Second from left is B.E. Andre, who became an Indian dealer and campaigned an ex-works 30.50 on the board tracks in the 1920s.*
**Photo courtesy of the B.E. Andre collection.**

# INDIAN ARCHIVE

Over the years the beautiful and graceful motorcycles Indian produced at its famous Wigwam have inspired photographers almost as much as they have inspired motorcyclists. Portraits of these magnificent machines create a visual history of the fabled marque that extends back to the company's very beginnings. We are proud to present a collection of this historic material, some of it unpublished, from Don Emde Productions, the June Cook Collection, and the Earl Bentley Collection.

Ralph Rogers, who envisioned an exciting future for the Indian motorcycle, appears to be contemplating its past. When Rogers took control of the company in 1945, production had declined to barely more than 2,000 Chiefs per year. A new four-cylinder—the X44 project—was in testing, and civilian styling treatments were being considered for the shaft-driven 841 military machine. Rogers shelved all these products in favor of entirely new designs, and even suspended production of the Chief to focus on the new product line. Photo courtesy of Don Emde Productions

*Floyd Emde aboard the Big Base Scout following his Daytona 200 victory in 1948. Photo courtesy of Don Emde Productions*

*The Big Chief, George Hendee, aboard his Indian "motocycle."* Photo courtesy of Don Emde Productions

*Oscar Hedstrom—the Great Medicine Man—with his engineering creation. Photo courtesy of Don Emde Productions*

*Gene Walker, pictured aboard a Powerplus, was a brilliant racer who arrived on the national championship scene in 1915. He won nearly half the national championship races in 1919, setting many new track records in the process. In 1920 he set a land speed record of over 103 miles per hour at Daytona Beach.* Photo courtesy of Don Emde Productions

Ed "Iron Man" Kretz became one of America's greatest champions aboard the Indian Scout, winning the Savannah 200 in 1936 and the first Daytona 200 in 1937. He was twice elected America's most popular rider. Photo courtesy of Don Emde Productions

*The colorful rider Albert "Shrimp" Burns aboard an eight-valve Indian. Later he used the side-valve Powerplus to become the first man to win a championship at over 100 miles per hour, beating the legendary Jim Davis, who was riding a factory eight-valve Harley-Davidson. Photo courtesy of Don Emde Productions*

*Ralph Hepburn won championships for both Indian and Harley-Davidson. Photo courtesy of Don Emde Productions*

*Bobby Hill of the Indian wrecking crew won dirt track championships aboard the Sport Scout into the 1950s, long after the motorcycle was out of production.*
**Photo courtesy of Don Emde Productions**

George Hendee in 1883 at age 17, displaying some of the many championship medals earned as a high wheel bicycle racer. The young Hendee was nearly unbeatable, winning 302 of the 309 races he entered throughout his career. Photo courtesy of the Motorcycle Hall of Fame Museum Archives, June Cook collection.

*The Big Chief George Hendee, who took Indian from an idea to motorcycling's dominant worldwide brand.*
Photo courtesy of the Motorcycle Hall of Fame Museum Archives, June Cook collection.

*Oscar Hedstrom, known as Indian's Great Medicine Man for his ability to pull performance and reliability from basic internal combustion engine designs. More than 135,000 Hedstrom engines were manufactured to power Indian and other early American brands. Photo courtesy of the Motorcycle Hall of Fame Museum Archives, June Cook collection.*

*Following his retirement from Indian in 1916, George Hendee devoted himself to raising cattle and volunteer work for the YMCA and The Shriner's Hospital for Crippled Children. Here he is seen at his country estate in his YMCA uniform. Photo courtesy of the Motorcycle Hall of Fame Museum Archives, June Cook collection.*

Erwin "Cannonball" Baker got his name from a journalist's comparison of his transcontinental record rides to the performance of the Cannonball Express. Not content with record runs across the United States, in 1916 Baker toured the Pacific, setting 16 records in Hawaii, Australia, and Tasmania, including a ride of 1000 miles in 24 hours. Photo courtesy of Don Emde Productions.

*Cannonball Baker aboard a Powerplus endurance machine. Baker began his career as a track racer, but was much larger and heavier than the other top riders of the day. Though successful as a racer, he found his real niche in long distance endurance riding. His exploits helped establish Indian's reputation for durability and reliability. Photo courtesy of Don Emde Productions.*

Screen star Jane Russell takes delivery of her new Indian in Santa Monica. Both Russell and her husband were given Indians to help promote the new Dyna-Torque models that were introduced in 1948. Officially, the gifts were in recognition of her efforts to promote safe driving among teenagers and other users of two-wheeled vehicles in Hollywood. Photo courtesy of the Motorcycle Hall of Fame Museum Archives, Earl Bentley collection.

Floyd Emde takes the checkered flag from the AMA Starter Jim Davis and wins the 1948 Daytona 200. Emde led the race from flag to flag, finishing 18 seconds ahead of Norton rider Billy Mathews. It was the last-ever win at Daytona by an Indian rider. Photo courtesy of Don Emde Productions

*Early bicycle pacers were sometimes two-person machines; one to steer and one to watch the bicycle racers, regulate the throttle, and try to keep the machine running. They were so notoriously unreliable, race promoters sometimes had as many as six on hand just to keep one running. Oscar Hedstrom set new standards for reliability with his pacer, thus attracting the attention of George Hendee. Photo courtesy of the Motorcycle Hall of Fame Museum archives, Earl Bentley collection.*

*Dressed to the nines, American racing stars Paul Anderson, Ralph Hepburn, Johnny Seymoure, and Jim Davis pose for the camera at an Indian dealership during a tour of Australia. The banner on the dealership would suggest that the year was 1924. Photo courtesy of the Motorcycle Hall of Fame Museum Archives, Early Bentley collection.*

***The Wigwam sees its end of days when the majority of the huge factory was razed in 1984.***
**Photo courtesy of the Motorcycle Hall of Fame Museum archives,**

# EXHIBIT GALLERY

A century after a bicycle maker and a self-taught engineer first mounted a small motor in a bicycle frame and launched one of the most famous brands in American motorcycling history, an exhibit at the Motorcycle Hall of Fame Museum told the tumultuous Indian story. "A Century of Indian, presented by Progressive Insurance" opened July 7, 2001. The exhibit used the machines themselves to tell the story of Indian Motocycles. Many of those historic bikes are chronicled in the following pages.

# 1905 INDIAN SINGLE

By 1905, Indian had produced over 1,000 motorcycles, and in that year some significant changes were made in the design. The rigid front bicycle-type fork was replaced with cartridge-spring suspension, and a twist grip throttle was introduced. Indian's standard color was blue. Red—or vermilion—appeared as an option in 1903, and green was added to the color choices in 1905. This 1905 Indian single is owned by Mort Wood.

# 1909 TWIN

With the introduction of the loop frame, Indian could produce heavier motorcycles with more powerful engines. A good example was the 61 ci., seven horsepower model introduced in 1909. These were the last of the Hedstrom-designed engines. Special 580cc versions of the twin were developed for racing at the Isle of Man. In 1911, Hedstrom personally accompanied the machines to the Island and supervised their preparation and maintenance. Indian swept the event, earning first, second, and third places. The motorcycle pictured is owned by Bruce Linsday.

# 1911 BELT-DRIVE SINGLE

Unlike many motorcycles of its era, the first Indian featured a chain drive to the rear wheel. The strength and reliability of this system were proven many times in speed and endurance competition, and are given credit to a large extent for Indian's victorious sweep of the Isle of Man in 1911. However, chain drive did not provide the smoothness in day-to-day operation that some people desired, and in 1909, Indian began to experiment with a belt-drive option. Indian offered belt-driven motorcycles from 1910 through 1912. The motorcycle depicted is an unrestored 1911 belt-drive single owned by John Housinger.

# INDIAN BOARD TRACK RACER

In the early part of the century, board track racing was enormously popular. It began on the small, steeply banked motordromes, which were not much larger than bicycle velodromes. The racing was fast, close, and exciting, but very dangerous. The darkest day for motordrome racing came at a track in Newark, New Jersey, in 1912 when Indian factory rider Eddie Hasha lost control, killing himself, another rider, and six spectators. Motorcycle racing was severely denounced by leading newspapers, including The New York Times, and the motordromes became known as "murderdromes." However, promoter Jack Prince, who had built most of the wooden tracks around the nation, also created some board tracks as big as two miles in length, intended for car racing. Motorcycle racing remained popular on these larger ovals, drawing tens of thousands of spectators. Motorcycles were capable of very high speeds on the boards. For example, in 1926 Curly Fredricks set a board track record of 120.3 miles per hour aboard a 61-ci. (1,000-cc) side valve Indian. Pictured is a 1912 eight-valve board track racer owned by John Parham.

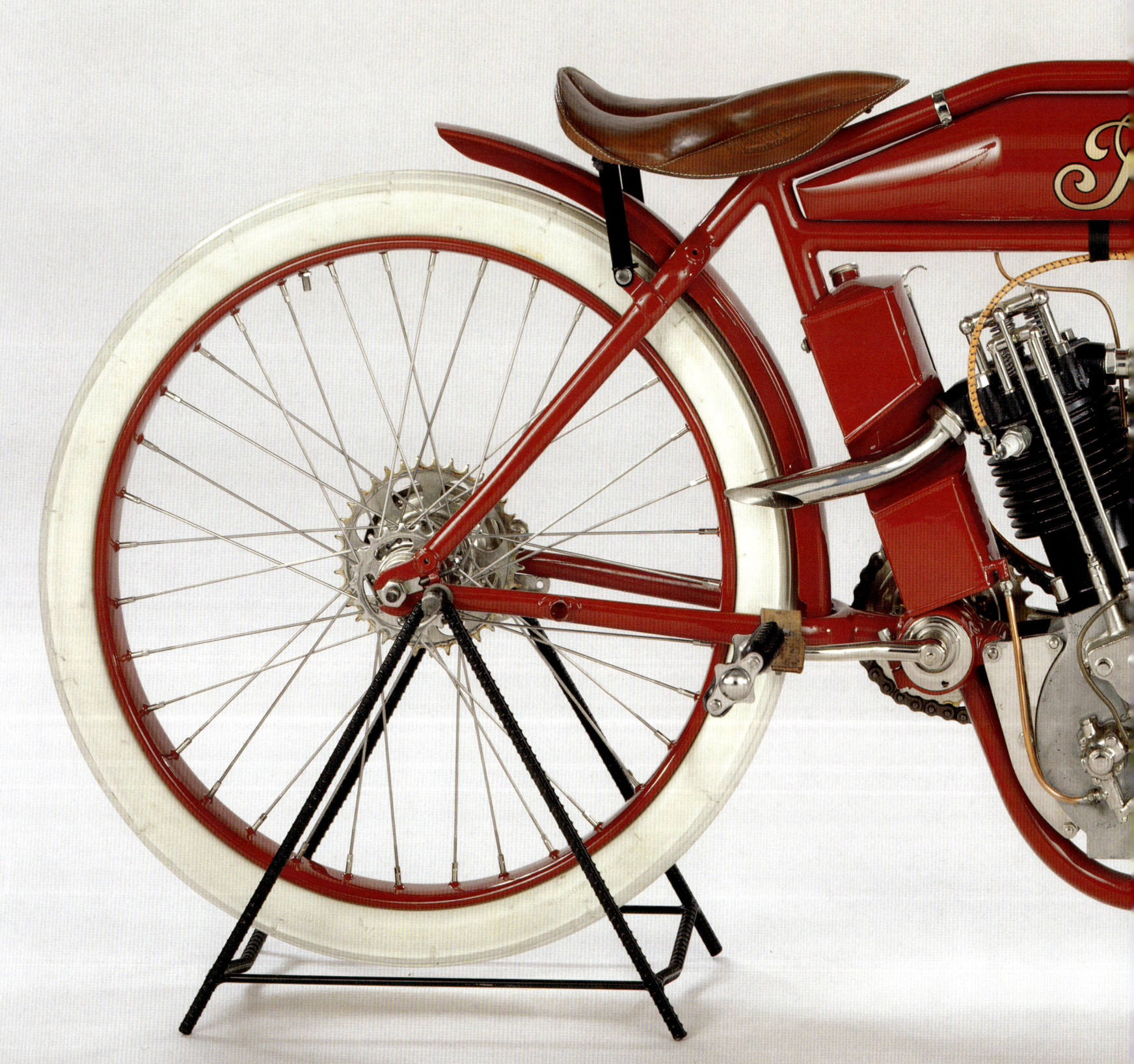

# VIRGINIA CREEPER 30.50 RACER

Following World War I, the sport of motorcycling was generally in disarray. The factories could no longer afford to fund big teams with special works racers. While board track racing remained popular in the 1920s, greater emphasis was placed on a 30.50-ci (500-cc) single-cylinder racing class, which it was hoped would be less expensive. Private builders often constructed their own racing machines, using works engines or components of works engines from the prewar era. However, Virginia Creeper, owned and raced by then Charleston, West Virginia Indian Dealer B. E. Andre, is a bona fide 1914 to 1916 four valve factory racer modified by Andre in the 1920's to keep it competitive. In the standard approach of the period, the frame was changed to lower the seat and accommodate a Scout fuel tank. Restored to the condition in which it was last raced, the bike is now owned by his son, Richard Andre.

# FIRST WORLD WAR MILITARY INDIAN

During World War I, Indian produced military motorcycles, based on their 1,000-cc Powerplus. The military model had flat fenders. It is estimated that approximately 20,000 military units per year were produced from 1917 to 1919. The 1919 model pictured is owned by Dave Uhl.

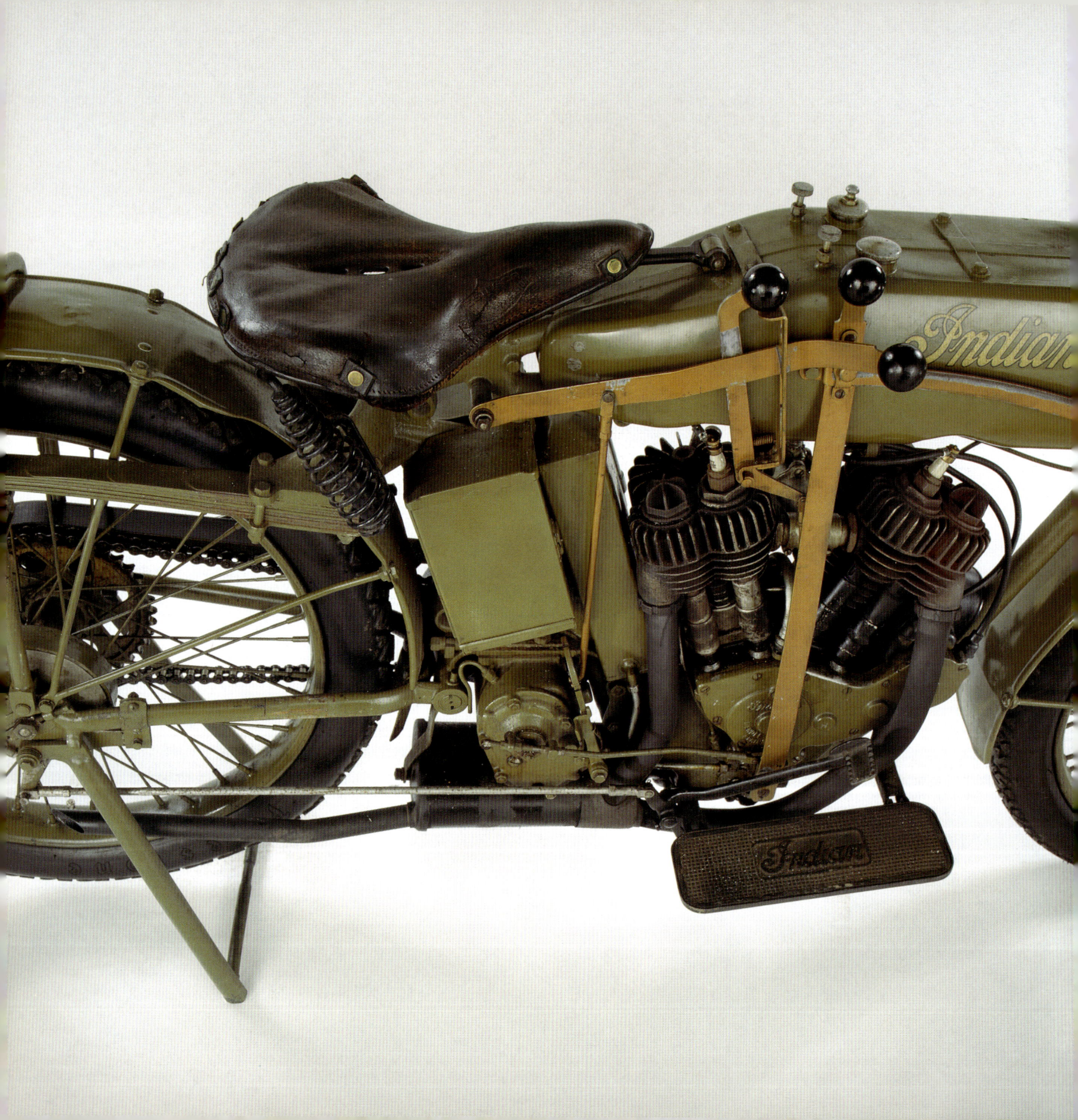

# 1923 BIG CHIEF WITH SIDECAR

When Fords and other inexpensive automobiles began to compete with motorcycle sales, American motorcycle manufacturers began to offer sidecars to improve carrying capacity and family comfort. Not only were they used as family transportation, but many businesses used sidecars for deliveries, or for carrying service tools and parts. In 1923 Indian enlarged its Chief from 61 to 74 cubic inches specifically for sidecar usage. This 1923 74 ci Big Chief is owned by Ernie Hartman.

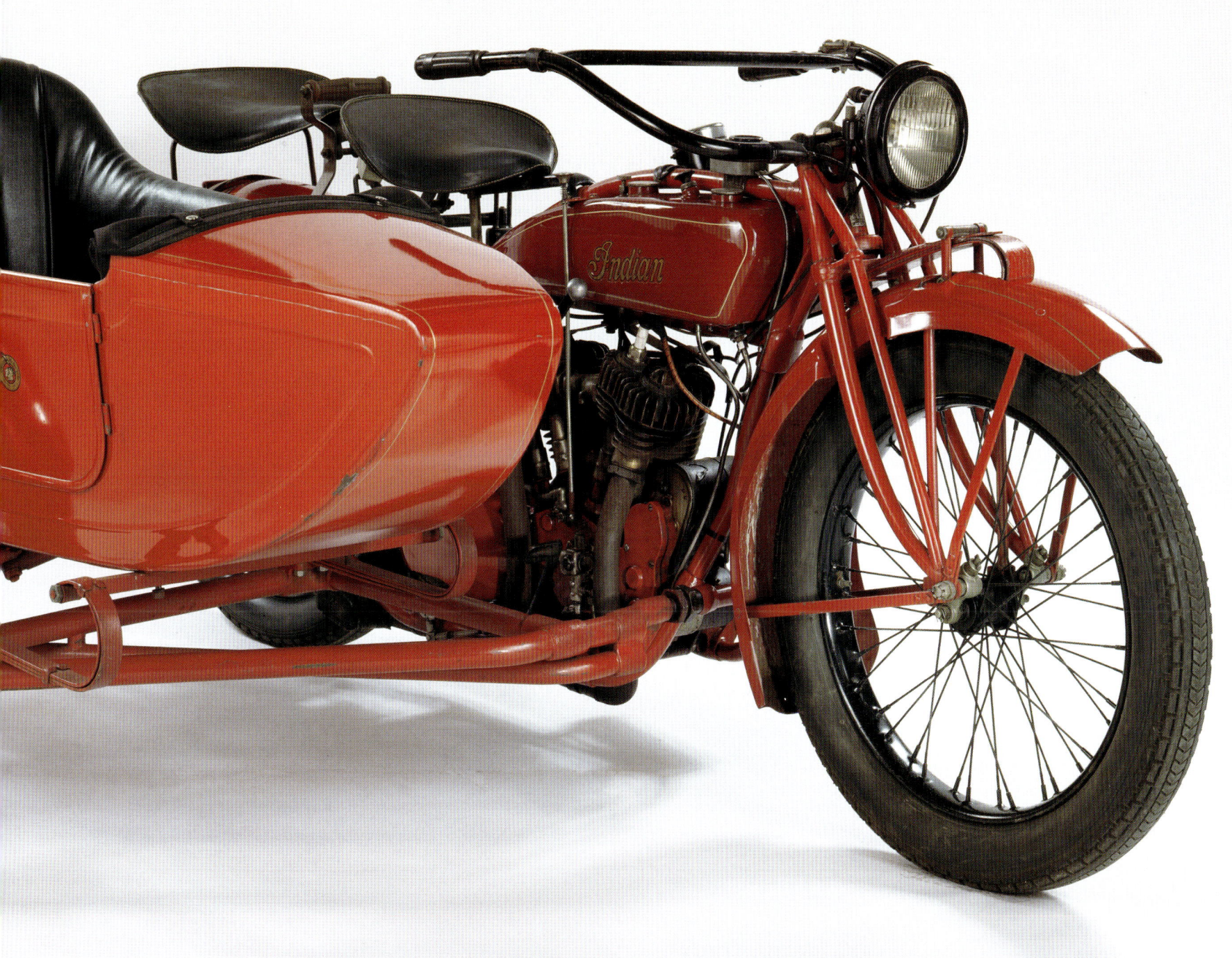

# 1926 PRINCE

Even after the unenthusiastic responses to the Featherweight and the Model O, Indian continued to try to break into an economy market with a small-bore motorcycle. In 1925, Indian again tried with its 350-cc Prince, a four-stroke side-valve single designed by Charles B. Franklin. It produced about six horsepower, could achieve about 60 miles per hour, and delivered 55 miles per gallon. With this motorcycle, Indian also hoped to improve its export sales, which had collapsed following World War I. Although the Prince was intended for a utilitarian, nonsporting market, its appearance in 1924 coincided with the introduction of a new 350-cc racing class, expected to improve safety and reduce the cost of racing. Both Indian and Harley-Davidson produced overhead-valve versions of their 350-cc singles designed for competition. The Harley was affectionately named the "Peashooter" for its small size, compared to the typical 1,000-cc machines of the day. Prince designer Charles Franklin responded with experimental overhead-valve and overhead-cam versions. The experimental overhead-cam model was never put into production. Pictured is Woody Carson's 1926 Prince LX2, a recreated Indian prototype using one of the few expeimental 21 cubic inch overhead camshaft engines in a modified Prince frame.

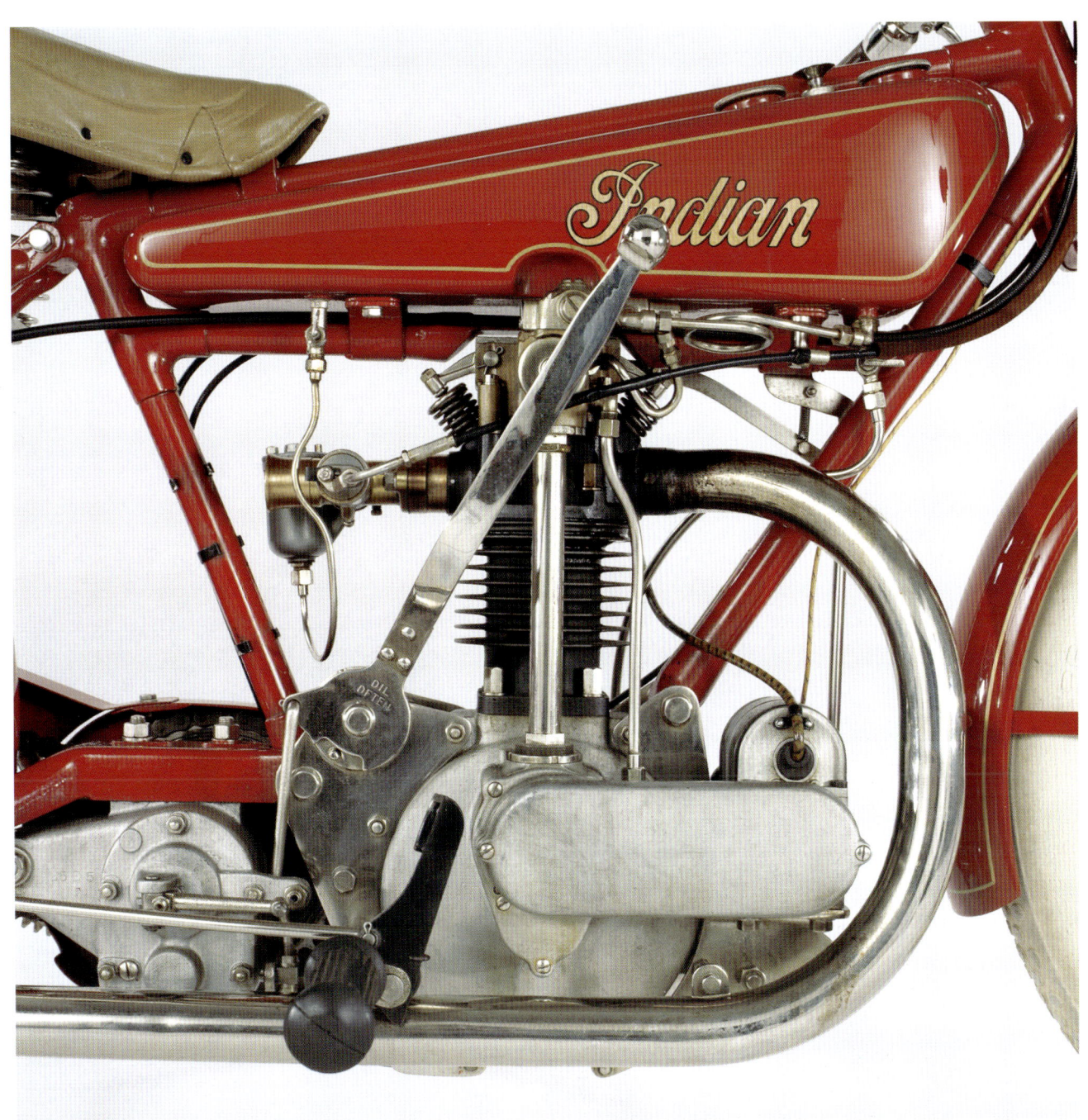

# BIG CHIEF

The 101 Scout, designed by Charles B. Franklin, was introduced in 1920 as a 37-ci side-valve V-twin. The compact and powerful engine provde so popular that in 1922 it was enlarged to 61 ci to replace the Powerplus engine powering the Indian Chief. in 1923 it was expanded again to 74 ci for the Big Chief, marketed with sidecar work in mind (note the sidecar mounting lugs on the down tubes ahead of the engine). The motorcycle pictured is a 1924 Big Chief owned by the Motorcycle Hall of Fame Museum.

# ED KRETZ SPORT SCOUT

The hard-charging Ed Kretz was the king of AMA Class C racing, initiated in the early 1930s. Kretz came into national prominence in 1936, when he won the Savannah, Georgia, 200-mile road race, but he is best known as the man who won the first Daytona 200, held on a beach course south of Daytona, Florida, in 1937. He was elected the AMA's most popular rider in both 1938 and 1948. Although he switched to Triumph in the later years of his racing career, his reputation is tied to Indian. Pictured is the restored 1937 Daytona winner, now owned by Ed Kretz Jr. It has appeared previously at the Motorcycle Hall of Fame Museum.

# INDIAN ARROW STREAMLINER

In the 1930s several motorcycle and automobile manufacturers began to experiment with streamlining. At the time, aerodynamics was still a young science and had been directed at making machines fly, rather than making them go faster on the ground. Working in secret, Indian's western states distributor Hap Alzina spent two years developing the Indian Arrow streamliner. Utilizing aircraft-grade spruce, balsa wood, and airplane fabric, the streamlined body was built like two halves of an egg shell bolted together around a rolling chassis. When "installed" in the Arrow, pilot Fred Ludlow was unable to get out of the machine without assistance. It was intended to seek a 61–ci record at the Bonneville Salt Flats in 1938. On September 24, Ludlow set a 45-ci record of 115.126 miles per hour, and followed it on September 26 with a 74-ci record of 120.747 miles per hour. However, both records were set aboard naked, unstreamlined motorcycles. With streamlining installed, the 61–ci machine proved unmanageable, beginning to wobble and yaw at approximately 134 miles per hour. Today the machine is owned by Harold Parks.

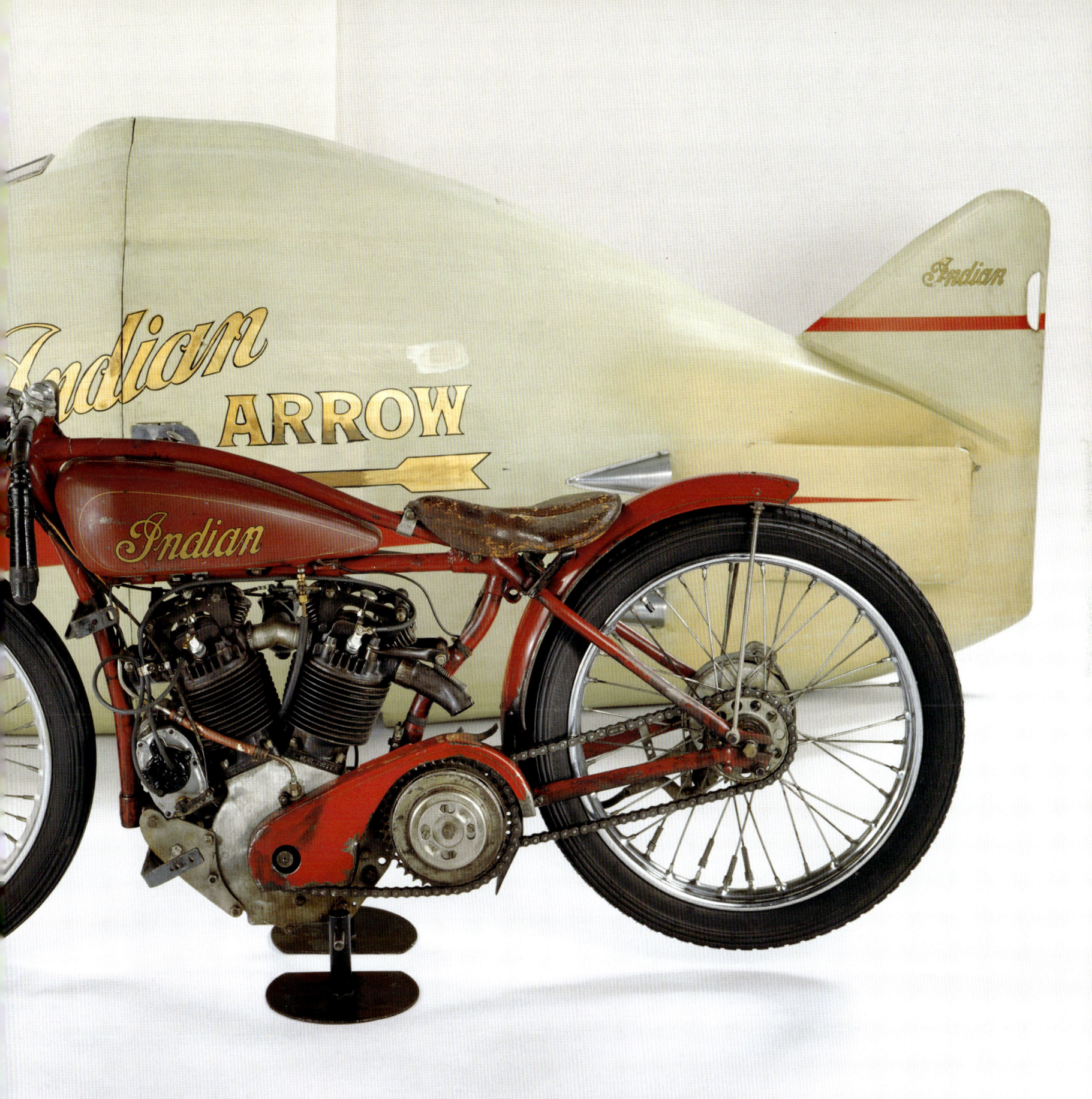

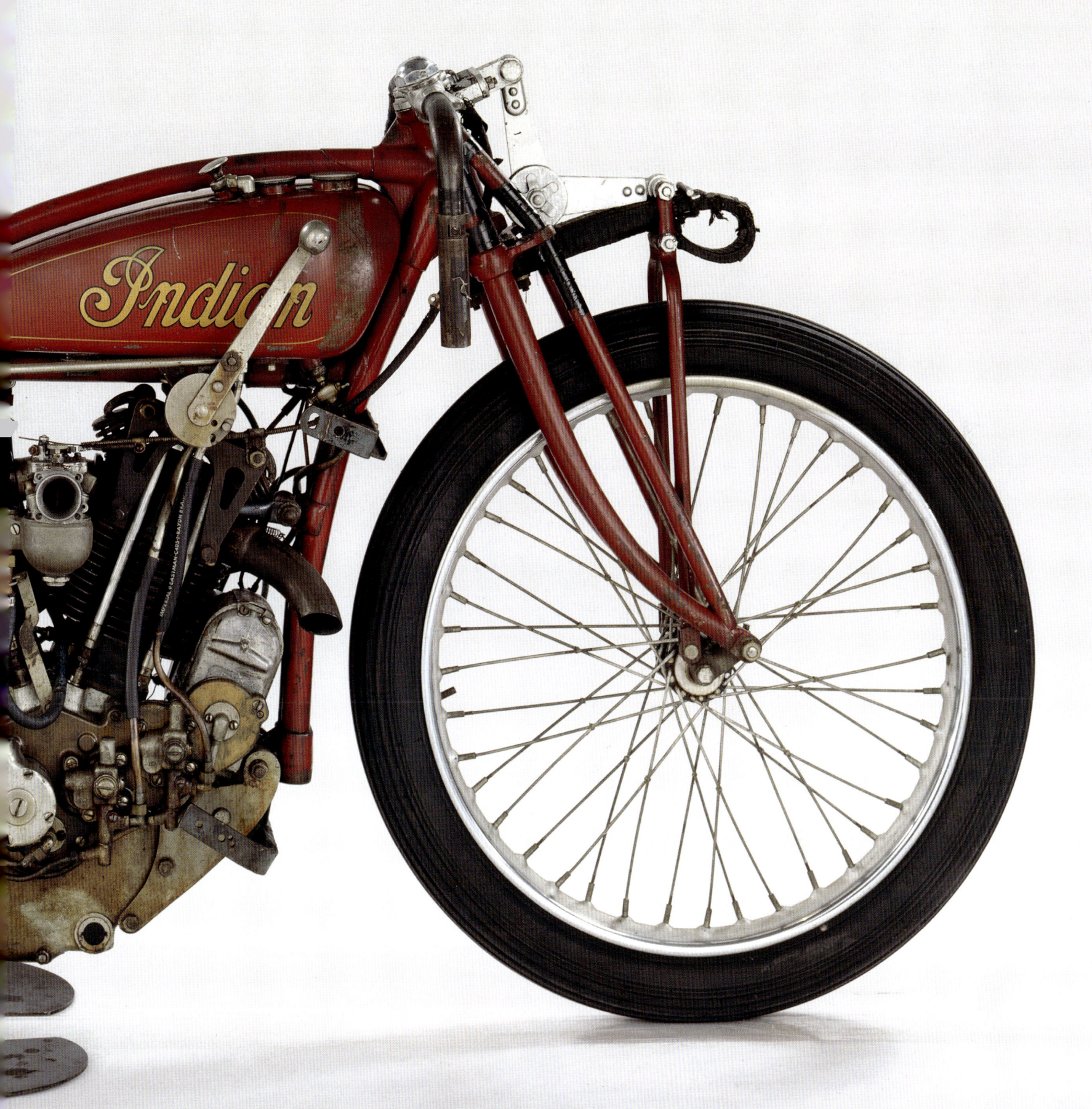

# 1940 SPORT SCOUT

What everyone knows today as the classic, full-skirted Indian appeared in 1940, a radical design departure by Briggs Weaver. It featured a long, streamlined tank, curvaceous deeply skirted fenders, and a large, beautifully shaped chain guard. Even the finning on the cylinder heads was sculpted to fit the smooth, sweeping lines of the motorcycle. It was to motorcycles what Auburns and Cords were to automobiles. The Chief had a plunger rear suspension, but the Sport Scout and the 30.50 had rigid frames. The 1940 Sport Scout pictured is owned by Curtis Poole.

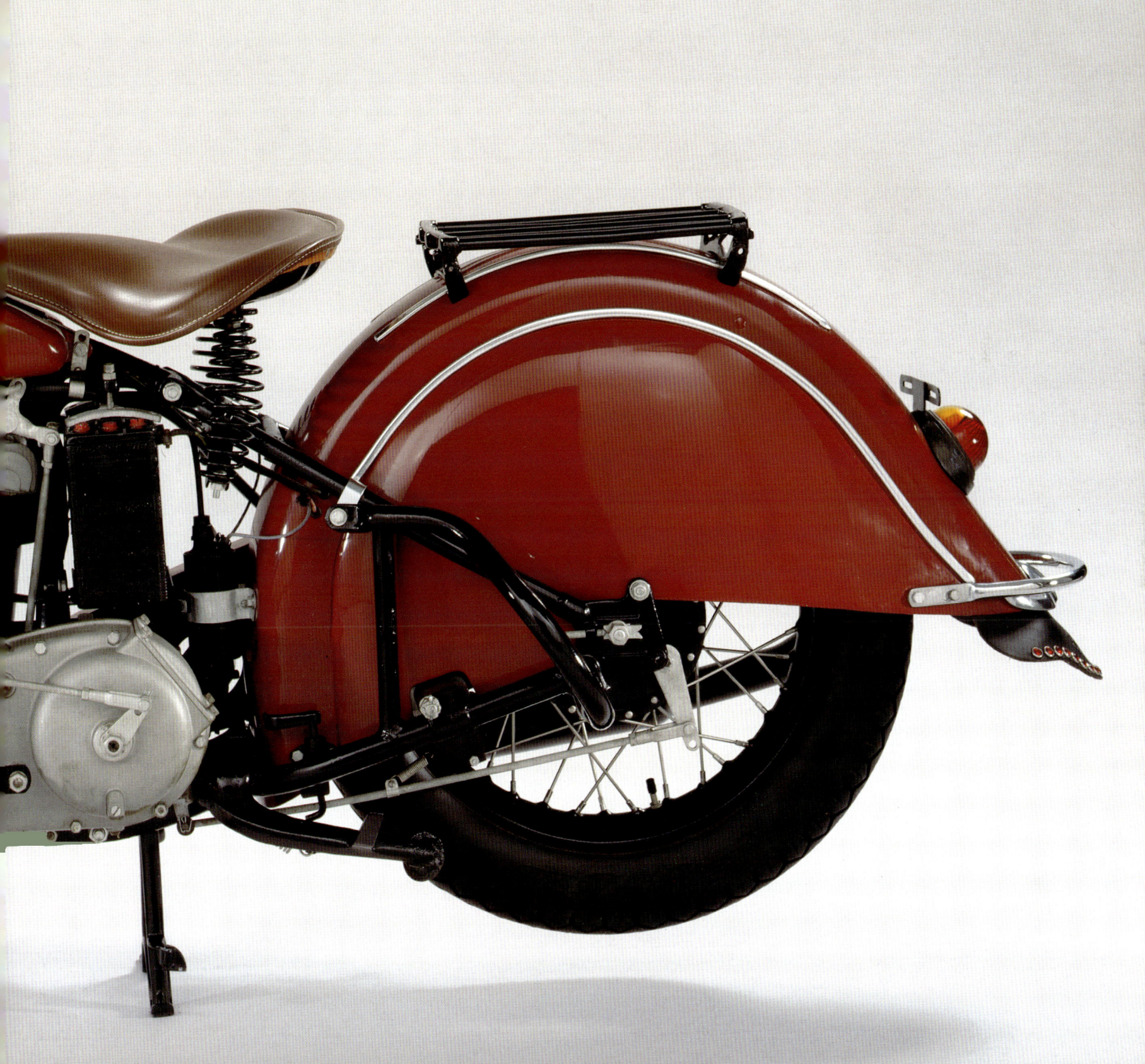

# 1941 INDIAN FOUR POLICE SPECIAL

Indian, Harley-Davidson, and Henderson all vied for law enforcement sales. Having a major city police force aboard your brand delivered prestige and high visibility. Though most Indian police bikes were based on the twin-cylinder Chief, some law enforcement organizations bought the Four. Pictured is an original, unrestored police Four used by the Marshall, Michigan Police Department. It is owned by Barry Stelford.

# 1947 INDIAN CHIEF

With its skirted fenders, the 1947 Chief captures the essence of Indian style. The 1905 Single and 1947 Chief represent the beginning and the end of the Indian Motocycle Company. When the green 1905 was built, Indian motorcycles were the most advanced machines of the era. Indian couldn't build enough motorcycles to meet customer demand. By 1947, the sidevalve technology used in the Chief was antiquated, and Indian was struggling to survive. The last Chief was built in 1953.

# 1949 SCOUT

Along with the single-cylinder Arrow, Indian introduced a 440-cc twin-cylinder Scout. It was a modern design and an attractive package, weighing only 285 pounds. With a foot shift and hand clutch like European and British motorcycles, Indian emphasized that it was easy to learn to ride, seeking to appeal to a new "gentleman motorcyclist" who might otherwise be intimidated by the traditional foot-clutch, hand-shift big twin motorcycle. The 1949 Scout pictured is owned by Greg Easley.

# INDIAN PAPOOSE

The Indian Papoose began life in wartime England as the Wellbike, designed for British paratroopers. After the war, John Brockhouse marketed a civilian version in England called a Corgi, then brought it into the Indian product line as the Papoose. It was powered by a 100-cc two-stroke Villiers Sprite engine. The Papoose shown is owned by Dottie Wood.

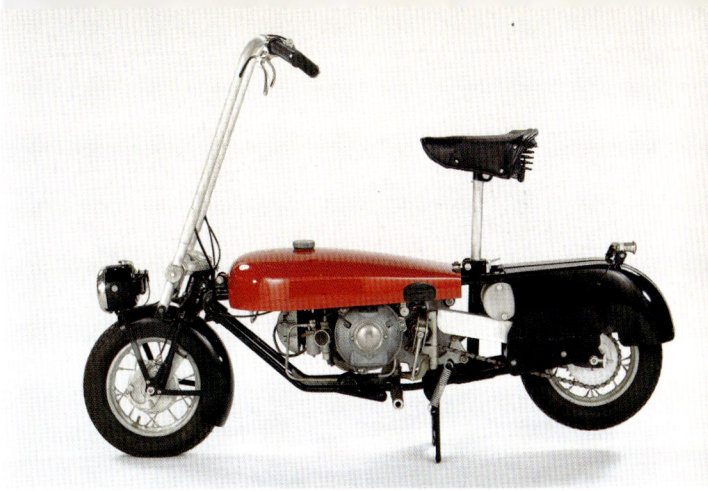

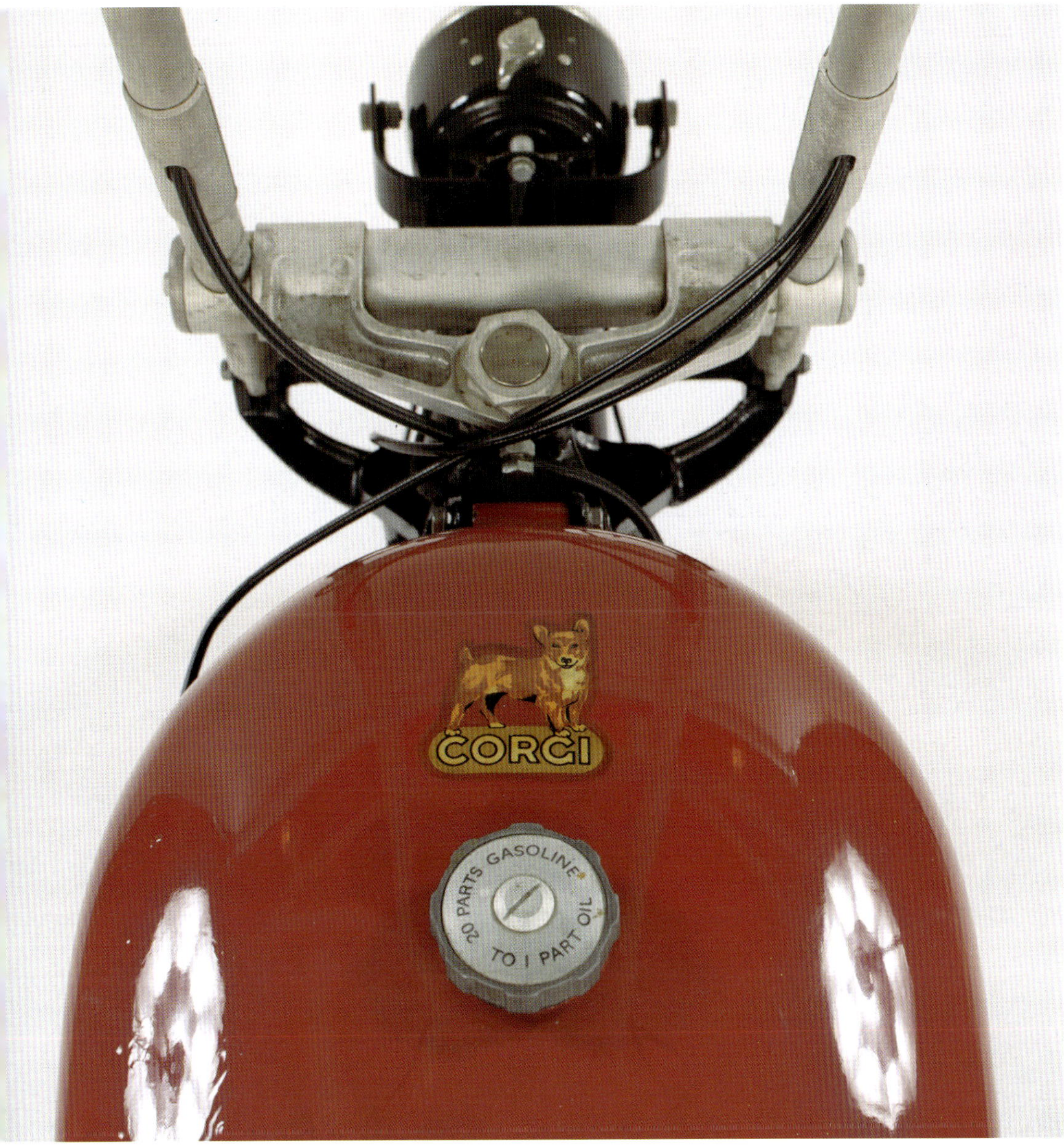
CORGI
20 PARTS GASOLINE TO 1 PART OIL

# THE CLYMER INDIAN

In 1968, Floyd Clymer began to import motorcycles under the Indian brand. They had either Velocette or Royal Enfield engines installed in frames made in Italy. It was learned later, during the great Indian trademark wars of the 1990s, that Clymer never had legal rights to the name and logo. He simply appropriated it for his use. The Clymer "Velocette" Indian pictured is owned by Arvid Myhre.

# INDIAN MINIBIKES

During the 1970s at least two companies imported foreign-made minibikes under the Indian brand name. This example, using an Italian two-cycle engine is owned by John York.

# GEORGE HENDEE
## IN HIS OWN WORDS

Published here, unedited and in its entirety, is a speech given by George Hendee, at age 65, on December 11, 1931, to the Springfield, Massachusetts, Rotary Club. In his own words, the Big Chief tells of his youth, his business career, and his public service following retirement. Beyond the historical facts, it provides insight into Hendee's ingenuity, optimism, and attitude toward work and his fellow man. The original typed manuscript of this speech has been generously donated to the archives of the Motorcycle Hall of Fame Museum by June Cook, niece of George Hendee, who inherited it in the effects of Edith Hale Hendee.

# How I Received the Title of "B.C."

*Address delivered before the Springfield Rotary Club, December 11, 1931*

The subject of my address as conveyed to you by the spokesman, "How I Received the Title of 'B.C.,'" was an intended misnomer and given to directly mislead you, fearing if the true title were known and you remembered the announcement made last Friday night, it might be the means of keeping many of you away from this meeting. With the present close contest on the Holyoke Club, this could not be tolerated, and only now I state my real subject, after you are all here and the doors locked. Therefore, let it be known that it is the story of my life that I am about to unfold, and I will pause at five-minute intervals for those who desire to quietly or otherwise steal away. Possibly as I proceed, you may be able to incidentally determine how I received the title of "B.C." Possibly some of you have erroneously arrived at the conclusion that it means Big Chump.

It is no secret, as it has already been published in the Roster, that I was born on October 2, 1866, in the small village of Watertown, Connecticut.

My parents, William G. and Emma Dwight Upton Hendee, were both of pure New England stock. My father was born in the town of Mansfield, Connecticut, and followed silk thread manufacturing during the major portion of his life. This was possibly influenced by the fact that Mansfield was the first town in the United States to take up silk manufacturing and the raising of the silk from the cocoon. My grandfather Hendee, when my father was a small boy, undertook silk culture, having erected a specially built building to house the worms. This building was fitted with trays to hold the worms and at feeding time, leaves picked from mulberry trees were spread over them. While it is true that silk worms will eat the leaves of grapevines, currants, etc., it is a very strange fact that they produce silk only when fed on leaves from the mulberry tree. The silk culture was a failure, because not enough mulberry leaves could be produced, owing to so many of the mulberry trees dying yearly from winter killing, and the silk culture was abandoned in this part of the country after two or three years.

My father's family was composed of five brothers, all of fine figure and of great strength, who lived to an average age of 87 1/2 years, my father dying in his 84th year.

My mother was born in Charlemont, Massachusetts, and was a fine specimen of womanhood, being tall, straight and well proportioned. In her family there were four brothers and several sisters. Her brothers were truly giants, not one of them being less than 6 feet 4 inches in height. From this, you can see that I started out in life with a most wonderful heritage, and while I did not have the choice of parents, it can safely be said that what little success I may have made of life, a large share can be credited to those who gave me being. A boy was never blessed with finer parents. They have both always been an inspiration to me. So therefore, let me here make a quotation that will apply to the lives they lived better than any words that I might express, and represents the principles that they tried to instill in me.

"To be strong and true; to be generous in praise and appreciation of others; to impute worthy motives even to enemies; to give without expectation of return; to practice humility, tolerance and self-restraint; to make the best use of time and opportunity; to keep the mind pure and the judgment charitable; to extend intelligent sympathy to those in distress; to cultivate quietness and nonresistance; to seek truth and righteousness; to work, to love, pray and serve daily; aspire greatly, labor cheerfully and take God at his word, this is to travel heavenward."

I can add that they always lived with courage, simplicity, and unswerving faith, and died in the hope of a glorious immortality. I am reminded of many teachings of my saintly mother. I have heard her often say "George, always keep good-natured in your battle with the ups and downs of life, keep your brow clear of those wrinkles running up and down, which always denote worry and care. The ones running across do not materially matter."

In later years I ran across the words of James A. Garfield, "If wrinkles must be written on our brow, let them not be written on the heart. The spirit should not grow old." No doubt that was in part what my mother tried to convey to me.

It is rather embarrassing to stand before you and try to impart what I have to say without appearing somewhat egotistical, and repeating at varying intervals the pronoun "I." You therefore must bear with me, for how otherwise can I tell the story of my life?

My boyhood was passed similarly to that of other boys who were active, restless, and full of life. I was unfortunate in not having the great benefit of being brought up with brothers and sisters. My only brother had grown to young manhood and had left home before I was born. I have always considered the loss of close brother and sister associations as a handicap, and I envy any child having enjoyed those privileges.

Nature endowed me in my early days with a most wonderful memory and I can recall many scenes and incidents which transpired even as far back as when I was 2 1/2 and 3 years of age.

My education was started at the age of five, and well I remember my first impression. My mother went with me and arriving early at the school, there was great noise and much confusion, which frightened me and quickly took away all desire to attend school. I gave my mother's skirt a pull and said, "I won't go to school." My mother gave me her kindly assurance. Order was soon restored, my courage returned, and from that time on, no boy ever enjoyed attending school better than I, and being healthy, I went for many years without being absent or tardy. I was not a blue ribbon scholar, but I always was able to pass the tests when the tests came.

From the time I was able to walk until I was 14, each summer vacation was spent on my uncle's farm in the high hills of Rowe, in northern Massachusetts. There, work was the order of the day, and I was kept going from early morning until nightfall at such tasks as my age would permit. Only on rainy days was the routine broken, when I could go fishing, a sport I have enjoyed down even to the present day. Here on the farm with its heavy duties was generated the endurance and stamina that were to stand me in good stead in many different ways in my after life. The neighbors, always curious as to when I had arrived at the farm, kept strict watch of my uncle's dooryard. A small flag pole was erected and immediately after arriving, I would jump from the carriage, pull up to the peak a small United States flag, which always remained flying until just before leaving. My last act was to pull down the flag, thus signifying to the world that I was no longer there.

In the year 1878, when I was 12 years of age, we moved to Springfield. My father accepted the position of superintendent of the Springfield Silk Mills Company, which occupied the buildings on Mill Street at the foot of Maple, where the Springfield Webbing Company is now located. I attended the Central Street Grammar School under that grand old principal Elias Brookings, graduated, and entered the old High School. One of my earliest boy associates at the Central Street School is none other than Frank Wakefield, one of our Rotary members.

Throughout my boyhood, I was always handicapped by being very large for my age, which was a disadvantage, as often much was expected of a boy of such size. It stood me in good stead, however, from the athletic side, as I was always most active in running, jumping, skating, and baseball. Playing once on the Central Street School nine, in opposition to the Chicopee Falls High School team, composed of boys far beyond our age, I saved the day in the last half of the ninth inning, with two out and the bases filled, by knocking out a home run. I had my first experience of being carried on the shoulders of my comrades.

One day during the summer of 1881, I was standing in front of our home at 239 Mill Street (and here is a strange coincidence, as that arrangement of figures, 239, was within a few years to constitute the world's record on a bicycle for 1 mile, and which stood for quite a length of time) and as I looked up the hill of Maple Street, I saw a sight that will forever remain with me. It gave me a thrill I cannot ever forget. Coming down the hill was a man seated, as it seemed, on a big wheel, with his legs hanging over a bar, making no sound and going at terrific speed. He sped by me as I stood there in open-eyed astonishment and no doubt with my mouth agape, until losing headway, he was obliged to take his legs down and then pedal himself away. This event without doubt changed the whole course of my life and led on to such little fame as the bicycle brought to me in the immediate years to follow. On partially regaining my normal conditions, I rushed into the house to tell my mother about the astounding miracle I had just beheld. Mind you, I had never even heard of such a vehicle. She said she thought she had seen something of the sort illustrated in some magazine. The contents of every book and magazine in the house were examined with feverish haste, until at last the illustration was found. A bicycle. Bi for two and cycle for wheel, or in other words, two wheels. My excitement had been so great that up to that time I had not realized that the apparition I had seen was supported on two wheels. I have always stated that this first sight of the bicycle changed my whole life's course, leading as it did from one thing to an other: riding, fancy riding, racing, business, and in later days to the motorcycle.

A few weeks later, through the kindness of a friend, I learned to ride. This bicycle was constructed out of an old wooden buggy wheel with a small wooden wheel in the rear, connected by a gas pipe to the front forks and handlebars. On this so-called backbone was fastened a cast-iron seat, which in your many falls over the top and into the dust of the roads had to be skillfully avoided, or it would strike you in the back of the head, which would add to your discomfort as you listened to the jeers of your companions. Late that fall a cousin visited us from Westfield, and allowed he had a second-hand machine, which he would sell for $45. My father was away from home at the time, and as I look back I can imagine the life my mother led until she finally gave in and the bicycle was bought. Let me say right here that at that time in our family, $45 was a small fortune, but the future proved it to be a fine investment. Well, with the bicycle came more worries for Mother. The bicycle must be exercised, and a trip to New Haven to visit my brother must be undertaken. That city was a full 65 miles distant by road, and the condition of the roads in those days made the trip really double the actual distance. The start was at daybreak one frosty morning in the month of November, and by continuously hard riding, I had reached North Haven as the shades of night began to fall. I had been told that the road from that point to New Haven was fine, wide, and smooth, and so it proved to be. But here is where the misery came in—the wind blew so hard over the salt marshes, striking me practically head-on. It would blow me over into the ditch, and over the top I would go. After several such flights through the air, which added greatly to my already tired conditions, I decided to hoof it. And hoof it I did those 9 long, weary miles into New Haven, pushing that machine. Finally after reaching the confines of the city, where the houses kept the wind off, I remounted and rode slowly but gaily up to my brother's house. Going to the side door, I rapped and my sister-in-law came and looked at this woebegone, dirty, dusty, clothes-torn specimen, not recognizing me at first. But after a moment she threw her hands up in the air and exclaimed, "Why Georgie Hendee, where did you come from?" With an effort, I threw my shoulders back and said in the best voice I could command, "Just rode down from Springfield on my bicycle." Needless to say, I did not ride back.

Many of you may remember and others of you have been told that in the old days of the high wheel and for a few years thereafter, Springfield was known the world over for its celebrated bicycle tournaments. It had the fastest track, the races drew the largest crowds, and it was the gathering place every September for all the great racing men of the world. These tournaments lasted three and four days. In the year 1883, a four-day tournament was in progress. On the third day, on which the 20-mile Championship of America was run, more than 32,000 people paid admission to Hampden Park. If you look up the population of Springfield at that time, you will find it was slightly above 35,000. Special trains were run from every point of the compass, and special Pullman cars came from many of the larger cities east of the Mississippi River. Practically every place of business in the city was closed on the afternoons of the races, and as far as it is known, these races were the only events ever held that caused the U.S. Armory to close.

Shortly after my return from New Haven, I was invited to join the Springfield Bicycle Club, which I did, becoming without superstition its 13th member. This club and I contributed much to the bicycling history of Springfield. I practiced fancy riding during the winters of 1882 and 1883 and became quite expert. At the great ball of the Springfield Bicycle Club held on February 22, 1883, in the old City Hall, I gave the first public exhibition of one-wheel riding without backbone or rear wheel. In those days it was an outstanding feat, and the newspapers heralded the fact with the caption "One wheel and the only man in the world that can ride it." It should have been "the only boy," as I was only 16 at the time. I had practiced in private, and when Henry E. Ducker, president of the club, announced after I had concluded my fancy exhibition, that I would now perform a feat never before accomplished, even he did not know what was about to happen. When I went out on the floor trundling the single big wheel by the handle bars, a loud shout of laughter went up. I took two or three steps, mounted the wheel and started around the hall. In a moment the silence was so great you could hear the floor boards of the hall creak. Having made three circuits of the hall, I dismounted, but the applause induced me to make two or three more circuits.

Now you see the merest child perform the one-wheel act without even handlebars. So onward moves the world.

I am getting ahead of my story. On July 4, 1882, the first bicycle race was held at Hampden Park, a 2-mile race for the championship of the Springfield Bicycle Club. By this time, the club had increased to 24 members. On the morning of the Fourth, I had received from the Pope Manufacturing Co. of Hartford a brand new 54-inch Standard Columbia Bicycle, weighing 65 pounds. On mounting it, I spent the morning in racing anything moving, from boys and dogs running to horses hitched to wagons or carriages that showed a desire to race. When the time of the race came, I was somewhat spent from my morning exertions. Even without this knowledge, I doubt if my competitors in the race, most of them men grown, gave me a thought as a possible winner. But when the dust of conflict was settled, it found me in the lead at the finish, well ahead of the second rider. I was truly launched upon a racing career.

My next race was in September, at the Agricultural Fair Grounds of Worcester, where I competed with Frank Moore, the 1-mile champion of England. I think it was his title that beat me as much as his ability to ride. In two heats of a 2-mile race, he came in ahead about 2 feet in the lead in each heat. The first great tournament at Springfield was slated a few days later, but here I was doomed to be defeated by Moore, again by the margin of 1 foot in the mile open race. This was the greatest race of the tournament, and the one in which all the prominent riders of America were entered. Jack Prince, the professional champion of America, had trained champion Moore for these races. Jack Prince saw in me the possibilities of a winner, with proper coaching and training—and let me tell you, I was crude, but I had plenty of speed, if I conserved it for the final sprint. He offered to train me for the One-Mile American Championship, which was to be run in Boston in the early part of October, and I accepted his offer.

On arriving in Boston and going to the street number given as the residence of Prince, I rang the bell. An English girl of about my age, about as comely and handsome as one would wish to see, came to the door. I was informed that Prince was out, but I should wait as he would return shortly. It was easy waiting, and taking her for Jack's sister, I was looking forward to a splendid two-week sojourn in Boston. These pleasant thoughts were cut short on Jack's return, when on entering and greeting me, he turned and said, "Meet the wife, this is 'Hannie.'" I learned much in those two weeks of hard training, the first I had ever had. How to conserve my strength for the final rush, the act of the ankle action in pedaling, the proper position on the bicycle, and the proper food for a training diet. Fourteen competitors lined up for the start of the race for the championship. I found my position between two of the larger men, who were mounted on bicycles with wheels much larger than mine, and although I was of good size, I must have looked "kiddish." Just before the pistol was fired for the start, one of the spectators said in a voice heard all over the field, "Look at the kid on a velocipede." The kid on the velocipede won the race and had placed in his possession the beautiful medal, representing the One-Mile Amateur Championship of America.

This medal was presented by the League of American Wheelmen, but it had to be won three consecutive times before becoming anyone's property. It had been won in 1880–1881 by Lewis T. Fry of Marlboro, Massachusetts, and would have become his property if he had won on the day it came to me. I was fortunate enough to win the championship in 1882–1883–1884, thus retaining permanent possession of the medal.

Winning the championship launched me fully into my racing career, which was to extend for a five-year period, during which I continued to hold the 1-mile championship and at different intervals the 2-, 5-, 10- and 20-mile championships. It was for the purpose of attending the Tournament of 1883 that A.H. Robinson, the English champion, visited America. The wonderful prizes offered for the four days of racing were displayed in one of the Main Street store windows. Quite a number of the prizes selected that year for the various races consisted of gold watches. On Robinson's arrival, he was taken down to see the prizes. After looking at them very intently for a few moments, he turned to his companions and said, "What in 'ell will I do with all the bloody watches?" The watches, however, became the least of his worries, as I defeated him in every race he entered. There was an aftermath to these races, however. After having been out of training for three weeks, during which Robinson had applied himself diligently to getting into good condition, he challenged me to a race for the 10-mile championship of America. This race was held on Hampden Park, November 3, 1883, drawing a great crowd and resulting in my possession of a most beautiful specially made medal to commemorate the occasion.

The champions of England attended in large numbers the tournaments held in Springfield in the following years of 1884 and 1885. None came in 1886, the last tournament held in Springfield for several years. It was at the end of this year that my racing career terminated.

I will not go into the details of those years, but in my five years of racing, I competed in 309 races. I won 302 of them and tasted the bitterness of defeat 7 times. Seeing nothing further to be gained by racing, it seemed natural that I should turn to selling the commodity that had brought me fame but little fortune. I therefore entered the commercial field, first as a traveling salesman, and then as manager of the bicycling department of a large sporting goods house in New York City. The yearn for Springfield was always with me, and in the year 1893, with limited capital, I opened a retail bicycle store at 478 Main Street, in the Walker Block. For three years, the business flourished. Not content to let well enough alone, and desiring to expand, in 1896 I took in a partner, acquired a factory, and entered into manufacturing Silver King and Silver Queen bicycles on a much larger scale. Time does not permit giving details that led to disaster, but owing to late delivery of materials, cancellation of orders, and our limited capital, an assignment was made on August 11, 1897.

Taking account of my financial condition after the assignment, I found I had $7 in money, owed $18, and was purchasing a house in the Forest Park District on installments. Certainly not a very promising outlook.

Seeing the man coasting down Maple Street hill on a high bicycle was the first turning point in my life, and right here came the second turning point. The assignee, knowing nothing about the bicycle business, easily disposed of all the readily sold assets, and in a short time was at a standstill. Seeing him about that time, I asked him what he proposed doing with the balance of the stock and plant. He said he would sell for a lump sum. I asked the price, and the one he named seemed most reasonable. I asked him to go through the plant with me, but instead he threw the keys toward me and said to take a look by myself. Taking advantage of this, I estimated by buying back the material he had sold that about 400 bicycles could be completed. From there, I went to one of the leading department stores on Main Street, whose buyer was a former president of the old Bicycle Club, and asked him if he wanted to buy 400 bicycles cheap. He allowed he did, and I induced him to put on his hat and coat and look at what I had to offer. Considering my proposition, he then and there gave me an order for the 400 machines, to be paid for on delivery at the store. I shall not tell you how I approached the assignee, but he allowed me free access to the factory on my promise that in 30 days I would place in his hands the amount named. I gathered together a few of the faithful men who had previously been in my employ, with the promise of wages sometime in the future. The machines were delivered, I received my pay and within the 30-day period, the agreed amount was paid over the assignee. With the plant in my possession and with money in the bank, in November 1897, the Hendee Manufacturing Company was incorporated under the laws of the State of Massachusetts, with a paid-in capital of $5,000. This company so founded, within a few years, was to become a great industrial institution in Springfield, employing more than 3,200 people, with the largest payroll at the time of any concern in the city.

The Hendee Manufacturing Company was originally incorporated for the purpose of manufacturing bicycles, and it continued so doing for several years. The Silver King and Queen bicycles dropped out of sight and the Indian Bicycle supplemented them. While we were successfully engaged, with an output of about 4,000 Indians a year, who should blow in but my old trainer, Jack Prince. "Blow in" is the only way of expressing his entrance, and anyone who knew him will agree that that expresses him exactly. Jack was full of the idea of building a wooden track for bicycle and bicycle paced racing. A deal was consummated, with Charlie Shean, another good Rotarian, and myself as partners. Jack quickly erected the track on West Street at the east end of the North End Bridge. This track was quite successful and was known as the Springfield Coliseum, and it was only torn down after its usefulness had ended.

Building this track was another turning point in my life, because it put me in contact with Oscar Hedstrom, the motorcycle wizard. Hedstrom had constructed two tandem-motor pacing machines that were well-nigh perfect, and with which he and his partner did much successful pacing and racing on the Old Springfield Coliseum track. The gas engine and the automobile were in their infancy, really in the experimental stage, when Hedstrom and I combined forces. In January 1901, he entered my employ to design and construct a motorcycle for road use. The actual work was started February 1, 1901. He designed the entire machine. He made the drawings, the patterns, and the tools. Doing all the machine work himself, he turned out the first perfected motorcycle on May 25 of the same year. This was a most wonderful feat, and it demonstrated his ability as a gas engine expert and a mechanic of outstanding ability.

With only limited capital—and it was limited—we had the nerve to start manufacturing the Indian Motocycle. Right here was another turning point. Had it not been for loyal friends who had confidence in us and the Indian, we could not have succeeded. The father of one of the Rotarians present here today came to us in one of our dark hours, and by financial assistance far beyond our worth, helped us over a rough spot.

Many times in those dark hours, I repeated the following: "For have there not been times, O God, when we peered into the gloom and the heavens were hung with black, and when life was well-nigh gone, we saw a light. It was the Star of Hope."

During the first years of our venture, we had many gloomy hours when even hope nearly vanished. But hanging on, we eventually stood on firm ground. You can get some idea of the depths through which we dragged ourselves during the first two years of introducing the Indian Motocycle when I say that at the end of the first year, red figures showed a loss to the extent of $25,000. In other words, we owed this amount, without funds to pay. Under these circumstances, it was hard to keep our heads above water, let alone ask for further credits, which were necessary if we were to continue. Our creditors had such faith that they not only stood by, but granted further credit. That was the only year as long as I remained with the company that our statement showed any loans unpaid or any indebtedness except current debts, and with a goodly cash balance in the bank at the end of each fiscal year. The business was a seasonal one, and during the preparatory manufacturing period, we were always large borrowers, and in the later years, it was not uncommon to borrow from $2 million to $3 million to see us through.

To illustrate the faith and loyalty given by my friends and creditors, let me describe the following incident, which took place during the second year of the Indian Motocycle, and the facts of which were not known to me for two or three years later. One of the concerns with whom we were doing a large volume of business was holding a directors meeting. The statement showed an item of $45,000, owed by the Hendee Mfg. Co. of Springfield. The president was asked who the Hendee Mfg. Co. was, and he replied, "Oh, that is George Hendee up at Springfield." Then the question as to the rating of the concern. The information: $5,000 capital, fair credit. The question at once occurred as to whether a firm with that meager capital and rating was entitled to such extended credit. The president replied that every bill was being discounted, and he thought it a good credit risk. The directors thought differently, and the upshot was that the president personally guaranteed the account. With backing like this, do you wonder we succeeded?

Our factory was originally located on the fifth floor of the King Block on Worthington Street, which was our office entrance and ran through and into the fifth floor of the Stacy Building on Taylor Street, where our factory entrance was located. We employed about 40 people at this time. Requiring larger and more convenient quarters, in the summer of 1904 we secured the old Technical High School building on upper State Street and moved in, I think, in the month of October.

From the first entry into manufacturing the Indian Motocycle and up to the time we moved to the State Street quarters, every energy in my being was put forth to bring the undertaking to a successful conclusion. Long hours, days of the week, and even health were not considered. I acted as purchasing agent, selling agent, financial man, credit man, advertising man, traveling man, shipping clerk, and demonstrator, and undertook any other odd job that came along. I carried every detail of the business on my shoulders and really thought no one could do as well as myself. A time came as the business grew when I found I could not carry all the load, and it was one of the hardest jobs of my life to lay aside the mass of details and assume only the larger responsibilities. I only did this after a struggle and fully realizing that others could attend to the details as well as I, if not better. I realized that no man could ever be a great executive who feels that he must, either openly or under cover, follow up every order he gives to see that is executed, nor that by so doing would he ever develop many capable assistants. During these years, I rode thousands of miles and entered all of the early Motocycle endurance runs, being a consistent winner in them all.

The building on State Street was 250 feet long, 50 feet wide, and five stories high. What we would ever do with all this space was a great quandary. Within a year we purchased the property with its frontage on State Street, Wilbraham Road, and bounded on the east by the railroad, and began an addition of 104 feet on State Street. Before this was completed, we began erecting the long building on the Wilbraham Road site. This was hardly completed when we purchased the property on the east side of the railroad, which contained the building known as the home of the Electron Mfg. Co. This building was remodeled. Then the property extending between State Street and Wilbraham Road to the east of the property mentioned was purchased. The houses were either torn down or removed, and the buildings extended up Wilbraham Road to Rutland Street, along Rutland and down State Street to the railroad, with bridges connecting above the railroad from the older to the newer buildings. A siding was provided for directly shipping and receiving goods and material. This gave a manufacturing floor space of over eight acres, and only in part met the needs of the expanding business. The plant was equipped with the latest modern and specially constructed machinery.

We now reach the year 1910. Without a dollar ever having been invested in the business except turning in the small original bicycle business, the company was capitalized, placing the company in the class where it belonged, with a capital of $2,600,000, and the highest rating given in the commercial reference books. During these years, the Indian Motocycle was known the world over, with 3,000 agents and 17 factory branches throughout the United States. We had a branch office in London, England, another in Melbourne, Australia, and a Canadian factory in Toronto. There was not a civilized country on the globe into which Indian Motocycles were not being shipped.

In 1912 another capitalization took place, and the capital increased to $12,000,000. During this year the great addition was erected in East Springfield, which is now occupied by the Rolls-Royce Company of America. This added 3 1/2 acres of additional manufacturing floor space, making a total of 11 1/2 acres. I was always proud of the construction, which is absolutely modern, and the fact that the plans were devised and the details laid out in our own engineering department. This year proved to be the peak year, with 32,000 Indian Motocycles built and delivered. During four months of the manufacturing period of this year, the average production ran 220 machines per day. After that, for several years annual production averaged between 25,000 and 26,000 machines.

I have spoken of loyalty and faith in the early days, but I cannot help at this time to speak of the loyalty and fidelity of everyone in our organization during the period I have just described. We were all like one great family, working for the common good. I do not think anyone was ever backed up by a more loyal staff. Throughout the large office force of more than 150 people, with its various divisions down through the 64 departments of the factory, a wonderful cooperative spirit prevailed. One of the outstanding factors was Frank J. Weschler, a former member of this club, who joined us soon after we moved to the larger quarters on State Street. Mr. Weschler, in the last few years of my office with the company, was treasurer and sales manager, and a few years ago became president and general manager. He resigned to take up an important position with what is now the Baldwin-Duckworth Chain Mfg. Co. It was in those days I was called "B.C.," being known throughout our worldwide organization as the Big Chief.

From my earliest childhood, the enjoyment of my life has been greatly enhanced by the undoubted faith and the untiring loyalty of nearly all with whom I have come in contact. That is what I have called friendship, and I have always tried, although no doubt have often failed, to carry on in kind. We help ourselves only as we help others, which is another way of saying as we Rotarians say, "He profits most who serves best."

On July 11, 1915, I took off the Indian War Bonnet, laid aside the tomahawk, sold out my entire interest, and retired from the Tribe. It has been a great source of pleasure to know that I was genuinely missed and my departure regretted. Taking up agriculture in earnest has given me a great kick and possibly will prolong my life. I am vitally interested in my herd of Guernsey cattle, which is becoming well and favorably known throughout the United States. And if you visit a certain restaurant on Main Street, you will hear my name called quite often, "one Hendee" meaning that Hilltop eggs are also well and favorably known.

I was overseas twice during the World War. My first trip was undertaken for business for Indian Motocycle in December 1914, when the war was in its early stages. I saw much of the war, as my trip took me to both England and France. It may be of interest that I came home on the *Lusitania*, on the last trip she made this way, as she was torpedoed on her return trip to England.

My second trip was for six months in the service of the Y.M.C.A., beginning in November 1917 and ending in May 1918. I had the pleasure of establishing for the Y.M.C.A. its postal telegraph and cable departments. During my services as postmaster, I had some most wonderful experiences, including many visits to the front, one time remaining in the front line trenches for five days and five nights. The last month in France, I had a military pass taking me both into the front lines and back areas wherever American troops were located, and I made the most of my opportunities. On my return trip home, I had the exciting experience of being on a ship attacked by a German submarine. While a torpedo was discharged at us, it went very wide of its mark. I was in Paris throughout the early bombardment of the Long Range Gun, and brought back a piece of the shell that burst in the Church of Saint Gervais on Good Friday afternoon, killing 75 of the worshipers and wounding 90 more. I saw the carnage wrought from the inside of the church on the following Easter Sunday morning.

In 1920, I took another trip to England and France and was able to go over the English and French fronts, and visit many of the scenes on the American front that had been viewed under entirely different circumstances during the war. I made another trip across the water and returned in 1922, completing my 23rd voyage. My first crossing was in 1888, and many of the ones to follow were on business, and a few were for pleasure. In computing the time consumed in my various crossings, I find I have spent more than a whole year of my life crossing the Atlantic Ocean.

You are all familiar with my activities during the past eight years, in connection with the Shriners' Hospital for Crippled Children. Let me end my discourse with a quotation that became my business creed, and which was instilled into the loyal staff of the Hendee Mfg. Co., and a message I hand on to you:

"I believe in the stuff I am handing out, in the firm I am working for, and in my ability to get results. I believe that honest stuff can be passed out to honest men by honest methods. I believe in working, not weeping; in boosting, not knocking; and in the pleasure of my job. I believe a man gets what he goes after, that one deed done today is worth two deeds tomorrow, and that no man is down and out unless he has lost faith in himself. I believe in today, and the work I am doing; in tomorrow, and the work I hope to do; and in the sure reward that the future holds. I believe in courtesy, in kindness, in generosity, in good cheer, in friendship, and in honest competition. I believe there is something doing somewhere for every man who is ready to do it."

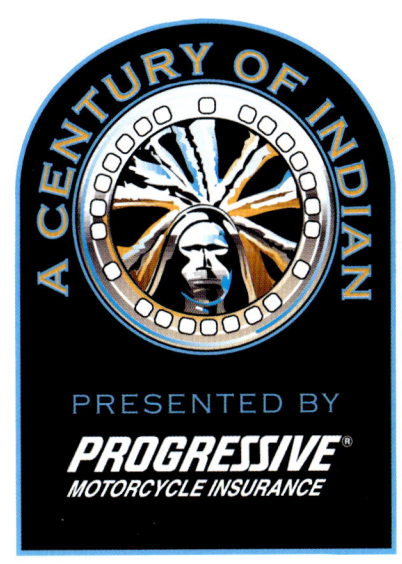

Progressive, America's #1 motorcycle insurance company, is proud to be associated with the Motorcycle Hall of Fame Museum, and the American Motorcyclist Association.

Progressive salutes today's motorcyclists and supports the preservation of the heritage of motorcycling.

# INDEX

Altoona engine, 26
Alvord, John F., 23
Alzina, Hap, 50, 134
Armstrong, Bob, 26
Baker, Erwin "Cannonball," 85, 86
Bauer, Louis E., 34
Baughman, Wayne, 65
Bigsby, Paul, 55
Brockhouse, John, 50, 51, 53, 66, 154
Clymer, Floyd, 51, 53, 64, 156
Cradle Spring frame, 20
Crocker, Albert, 54, 55
du Pont, E. Paul, 35–37, 39, 40, 42, 65
du Pont, Francis, 35, 36
Emde, Floyd, 51, 73, 88
Excelsior, 33, 34
Franklin, Charles, 20, 28, 30, 32, 35, 40, 42, 124, 128
Gustafson, Charles Jr., 29, 30
Gustafson, Charles Sr., 20, 29, 30
Harley-Davidson, 16, 18, 23, 27–29, 33, 37, 42, 43, 46, 54, 65, 124
Hasha, Eddy, 21, 22, 110
Hedstrom, Oscar, 10, 11, 13, 20, 22, 23, 30, 60, 75, 83, 88, 100
Hendee, George, 10, 16, 17, 23, 29, 60, 74, 81, 82, 84, 88, 160–166
Henderson, William, 22, 34
Hepburn, Ralph, 79

Hill, Bobby, 80
Hill, Jimmy, 40, 48
Hodgdon, Ted, 38
Hosley, Loren E. ("Joe"), 36, 37, 39, 40
Indian Arts and Crafts Act, 65
Indian Models, General
    Ace, 22, 34
    Arrows, 35, 47, 48, 134
    Board track racers, 110
    Century Chief, 65
    Chiefs, 43, 48, 50, 52, 56
    Clymer Indian, 156
    Dyna-Torque lightweights, 55
    Enfield Indians, 57
    Featherweight, 28, 29
    First World War Military Model, 118
    Four, 39, 47
    Indian Motorcycling Company (present-day) models, 66
    Minibikes, 158
    Model 640B, 47
    Model 841, 47, 56
    Model O, 28, 29
    Papoose, 154
    Powerplus (Standard), 33, 78
    Prince, 28, 29
    Prototype motor-bicycle, 11
    Scouts, 33, 36, 40, 47, 48, 128,
    Torque Four, 58

    Upside Down Four, 30
    Warrior TT, 51, 66
Indian Models, Specific
    1904 Single, 11
    1905 Single, 94
    1906 Tandem, 12
    1906 Tri-Car, 12
    1906 Tricycle, 12
    1906 Triplet, 12
    1906 Van, 12
    1908 sport bike ("monkey-on-a-stick"), 17, 18
    1909 Twin, 100
    1911 Belt-Drive Single, 106
    1914 Hendee Special, 16, 22
    1916 Featherweight, 19, 31
    1916 Powerplus, 20
    1917 Model O, 19, 31
    1920 Scout, 32
    1922 Chief, 32
    1923 Big Chief (with sidecar), 33, 122
    1926 Prince, 124
    1927 Factory Hillclimber, 26
    1927 Police Special, 33
    1928 101 Scout, 32
    1929 Four, 22
    1939 Traffic Car, 40
    1940 Sport Scout, 140

    1941 Indian Four Police Special, 144
    1946 Chief, 44, 46
    1947 Chief, 148
    1948 Model 648 Scout ("Big Base" and "Daytona" Scout), 50, 51
    1949 Arrow, 52
    1949 Scout, 150
    1950–1951 Warrior, 66
    Virginia Creeper 30.50 Racer, 114
    X44 prototype, 56
Kretz, Ed "Iron Man," 50, 77
Labriola, Lonnie, 65
Lemon, Arthur, 34
Mitzel, Howard, 26
Powerplus (engine), 30
Rogers, Ralph B., 42, 46–48, 50, 54, 55, 68, 72
Schwinn, Ignaz, 22, 34
Sidecars, 14
Silver Arrow outboard motor, 36
Stovkis, Jean and Paul, 47
Umpqua Indian Tribe, 65
Walker, Gene, 76
Weaver, Briggs, 30, 39, 40, 42, 43, 47, 48, 68
Wells, William H., 20
Weschler, Frank J., 23
Zanghi, Philip S., 64, 65